Canva Cookbook

Unlock the full potential of Canva with practical recipes
for creating stunning visuals effortlessly

Barbara Tulissi

Canva Cookbook

Group Product Manager: Rohit Rajkumar

Publishing Product Manager: Tanisha Mehrotra

Book Project Manager: Sonam Pandey

Senior Editor: Hayden Edwards

Technical Editor: Simran Ali

Copy Editor: Safis Editing

Indexer: Manju Arasan

Production Designer: Shankar Kalbhor

DevRel Marketing Coordinator: Anamika Singh and Nivedita Pandey

First published: January 2025

Production reference: 1101224

Published by Packt Publishing Ltd.

Grosvenor House

11 St Paul's Square

Birmingham

B3 1RB, UK

ISBN 978-1-80107-530-5

www.packtpub.com

To the classrooms that have become my second home, and to the brilliant young minds that grace them. Your thirst for learning and your unwavering spirit continue to inspire me, day after day. This book is for you, the next generation of designers.

– Barbara Tulissi

Contributors

About the author

Barbara Tulissi is an Italian designer who ditched her career in finance for the world of creative magic. Fueled by curiosity and a passion for empowering others, Barbara traded spreadsheets for design tools, becoming a master of both the classic Adobe Suite and the user-friendly phenomenon, Canva.

Today, Barbara's not just a designer, but a Canva Ambassador (Canvassador), spreading the gospel of design accessibility to young minds in classrooms, as well as to brands around the globe. Whether it's delivering practical takeaways at workshops or motivating and sparking discussions as a public speaker, Barbara's infectious enthusiasm makes learning fun and empowering.

I am deeply grateful to Hayden for his editorial expertise and unwavering patience. His guidance was instrumental in bringing this book to life. I would also like to thank my loving family for supporting and motivating my dreams, including my sister, Veronica, whose unwavering determination has always inspired me to strive for excellence. Finally, a special thanks to Artur for always joining me on my daydreams.

About the reviewers

Beatriz Moreno del Castillo is a marketing strategist, design expert, official Canva Content Creator, and founder of Violetwave Studio. With over a decade of experience in hospitality, working with brands such as NH Hotel Group and Pyramid Global Hospitality, she specializes in impactful brand communication, simplifying complex design processes and empowering teams to create visually compelling narratives while making design accessible.

For Beatriz, design is more than aesthetics—it's about creating empathetic, innovative, and functional solutions. Her unique blend of creativity and strategy has made her a trusted advisor for brands seeking meaningful audience connections.

Laura Goodsell is an award-winning creative designer, Canva creator, and Canvassador, helping small business owners to understand and utilize Canva for their own branding, social graphics, and digital products.

Building her business around her young family, Laura's mission is to use her skill set and help small business owners to have a head start by equipping them with the skills they need to create and grow their business through her YouTube channel, Canva graphics, and low-cost Canva design membership.

Parvathy Suresh is a skilled bioinformatician with a deep passion for design and creative writing. With a background in computational biology, she applies her analytical mindset to her scientific work while channeling her creative energy into design and storytelling. Her diverse interests allow her to bridge the gap between technical and creative fields, and she excels in both scientific research and artistic pursuits.

Table of Contents

Preface   xiii

1

Introducing Canva and Its Interface   1

Technical requirements	2	Single project interface	9
Discovering Canva's main interfaces	2	Create a design button	11
Canva search bar	3	Incorporating external resources and reviewing Canva limits	12
Visual Suite	4		
Templates	4	Implementing useful shortcuts	16
Brand Hub	6	Summary	16

2

Creating Your Brand and Shaping It in Canva   17

Creating your brand	17	Mood board	32
Day 1: Scope	19	Elements	34
Day 2: Vision	20	Color	34
Day 3: Mission	21	Fonts	38
Day 4: Values	24	Icons, images, and illustrations	41
Creating a brand archetype	28	Brand Hub	42
Developing your brand visual identity in Canva	32	Summary	47

3

Personalizing Your Social Media Presence   49

Crafting your brand's tone of voice   50
Getting ready   51
How to do it…   51

Improving your profile picture   53
How to do it…   53
There's more…   56

Creating an Instagram grid mockup   56

Getting ready   56
How to do it…   57
There's more…   62

Designing social covers for Facebook, LinkedIn, and YouTube   63
How to do it…   65

4

Crafting Engaging Social Content   71

Taking a single social media post to the next level   72
Getting ready   72
How to do it…   73

Creating a carousel post   78
How to do it…   79
There's more…   84

Creating an animated swipe-bounce effect for your carousel   84
Getting ready   84
How to do it…   84

Creating a collage post layout   86
How to do it…   86

Creating a mosaic effect for Instagram   88
How to do it…   88

Creating a social media story   90
Getting ready   91
How to do it…   92

Creating a meme   93
How to do it…   94
There's more…   96

5

Creating Impactful Presentations   97

Creating a presentation for a client   97
Getting ready   98
How to do it…   98
There's more…   103

There's even more…   107

Creating a presentation from a document   107
How to do it…   108

See also	109	Getting ready	117
		How to do it...	117
Visualizing data better in your		How it works...	123
presentations	**109**	There's more...	124
Getting ready	110		
How to do it...	110	**Presenting presentations in Canva**	**124**
		How to do it...	125
Using infographics in your		There's more...	131
presentations	**112**		
How to do it...	112	**Importing, exporting, and sharing**	
There's more...	116	**your presentations**	**131**
		Getting ready	131
Utilizing animations in your		How to do it...	131
presentations	**117**		

6

Crafting Captivating Videos — 137

Defining your video's purpose and		**Generating subtitles**	**158**
message (part 1)	**138**	How to do it…	158
How to do it…	138		
There's more…	141	**Creating GIFs**	**161**
		How to do it…	161
Structuring and creating your			
video (part 2)	**142**	**Creating a label in Canva**	
Getting ready	142	**and CapCut**	**164**
How to do it…	145	Getting ready	164
		How to do it…	165
Animating your video (part 3)	**150**		
Getting ready	150	**Editing videos with Canva's AI**	**169**
How to do it…	150	Getting ready	170
		How to do it…	170

7

Mastering Eye-Catching, Stop-Scrolling Ads — 173

Defining your ad's objective and		**Finding references to get inspiration**	**175**
target audience	**174**	How to do it…	176
How to do it…	174		

Tailoring ad formats for different platforms	178	There's more…	192
		There's even more…	194
How to do it…	179	**Utilizing CTAs effectively**	**195**
Crafting stop-scrolling ads	**184**	How to do it…	196
How it works…	185	There's more…	197

8

Developing Effective Marketing Documents   199

Creating a digital business card	200	Creating a template for invoices and quotes	213
How to do it…	200		
There's more...	203	How to do it…	213
Transforming an event flyer	**204**	**Creating an email signature**	**216**
Getting ready	204	Getting ready…	216
How to do it…	207	How to do it…	216

9

Ensuring Accessibility and Inclusivity in Your Designs   223

Reviewing the WCAG	224	How to do it…	231
		There's more…	233
Creating readable text and typography	225	**Enabling captions on videos and audio**	**234**
Getting ready	225		
How to do it…	226	How to do it…	234
There's more…	230	**Creating images using AI**	**236**
Using alt text for images and graphics	**231**	How to do it…	237

10

Designing Print-Ready Materials   241

Resizing your Canva project, ready for print	242	How to do it…	243
		Getting mock-ups for printing	**249**
Getting ready	242		

How to do it…	250	Exporting your design as a PDF	260
Using the Canva Print service	**253**	Getting ready	260
Getting ready	254	How to do it…	260
How to do it…	254	There's more...	264

11

Unlocking the Power of Magic Studio 265

Transforming your pictures with Magic Edit (Free)	**267**	**Generating brand-new illustrations with AI (Pro)**	**279**
How to do it…	267	How to do it…	280
Removing backgrounds (Pro)	**269**	**Writing with AI (Pro)**	**282**
How to do it…	269	How to do it…	283
Grabbing objects within a picture (Pro)	**271**	**Extracting text from images (Pro)**	**286**
How to do it…	271	How to do it…	286
Erasing objects within a picture (Pro)	**273**	**Extracting video highlights (Pro)**	**288**
How to do it…	273	How to do it…	289
Expanding your pictures (Pro)	**275**	**Transforming existing elements (Free)**	**291**
How to do it…	275	How to do it…	291
Resizing your content (Pro)	**277**	**Animating your designs (Pro)**	**293**
How to do it…	277	Getting ready	293
		How to do it…	293

Index 295

Other Books You May Enjoy 302

Preface

Canva is a powerful and intuitive design platform that has revolutionized the way we create visual content. From social media posts and presentations to marketing and printed materials, Canva provides a wide range of tools and templates to help users of all skill levels bring their creative visions to life.

The *Canva Cookbook* takes this user-friendly platform to the next level, providing a comprehensive guide to harnessing the full potential of Canva. It starts with how to create a brand, before delving into recipes, instructions, and practical tips to help you create stunning visuals that captivate your audience.

By the end, the *Canva Cookbook* will be your go-to resource for mastering this versatile tool and elevating your design game.

Who this book is for

This book is aimed at passionate designers with a basic understanding of Canva who want to use the platform to elevate their visual communication skills and create engaging, creative projects. Specifically, this book focuses on entrepreneurs who would like to elevate their design skills to help develop a personal or professional brand. This book is also useful for graphic designers, social media managers, and content creators who want to align their designs with an already-established brand.

What this book covers

In *Chapter 1*, *Introducing Canva and Its Interface*, we'll dive into the heart of Canva: its intuitive interface. We'll explore the layout, key features, and essential tools that will empower you to create stunning designs.

In *Chapter 2*, *Creating Your Brand and Shaping It in Canva*, you'll learn how to craft a strong brand identity by defining your brand's scope, vision, mission, and values. We'll explore the most common brand archetypes, and guide you through the process of creating a brand style guide that will ensure consistency across all your marketing materials.

In *Chapter 3*, *Personalizing Your Social Media Presence*, you'll learn how to create a cohesive and visually consistent brand identity across all your social media platforms.

In *Chapter 4, Crafting Engaging Social Content*, we'll explore strategies to craft engaging social media profiles and posts that resonate with your audience.

In *Chapter 5, Creating Impactful Presentations*, you'll learn how to design captivating presentations that inform, inspire, and engage your audience. We'll explore the art of storytelling, the power of visuals, and the importance of effective communication to create presentations that leave a lasting impression.

In *Chapter 6, Crafting Captivating Videos*, you'll discover how to create stunning videos using Canva's video editing tools, including how to add text and music. You'll also learn how to create GIFs and generate subtitles, and how to utilize Canva with Capcut to create video labels.

In *Chapter 7, Mastering Eye-Catching, Stop-Scrolling Ads*, you'll learn how to design attention-grabbing ads that stop users from scrolling and drive up engagement.

In *Chapter 8, Developing Effective Marketing Documents*, you'll learn how to create professional and persuasive marketing documents using Canva, including flyers and invoices.

In *Chapter 9, Ensuring Accessibility and Inclusivity in Your Designs*, we'll explore the importance of creating inclusive designs that are accessible to everyone. We'll discuss key accessibility guidelines, as well as Canva's Design Accessibility Checker, alternative text, and captions.

In *Chapter 10, Designing Print-Ready Materials*, we'll dive into the world of print design and learn how to prepare your Canva designs for professional printing, including how to use Canva's print service.

In *Chapter 11, Unlocking the Power of Magic Studio*, you'll discover the magic of Canva's AI features to speed up and elevate your creative projects to new heights.

To get the most out of this book

Software/hardware covered in the book	Operating system requirements
Canva	Canva works on your browser and allows you to save projects directly in the cloud. You do not need to download the Canva app for your laptop; however, I do recommend the app when using a mobile.

This book will largely cover the free Canva features; however, we will be discussing some of the Canva Pro features. Having the paid subscription helps you work faster and smarter but, when possible, I will give you some free alternatives to the Pro features.

Accessing the book's links

In this book, you will find some useful resources that I will link to in every chapter. You can also find them all here, so save this link for later: `https://caffecanva.my.canva.site/barbaratulissi`.

Conventions used

There are a number of text conventions used throughout this book.

Bold: Indicates a new term, an important word, or words that you see onscreen. For instance, words in menus or dialog boxes appear in **bold**. Here is an example: "In your project, click **File** and select **Show rulers and guides**"

`Code in text`: Indicates folder names, filenames, file extensions, pathnames, and user input. Here is an example: "Navigate to Canva's home page and search for `Infographic` in the search bar."

> **Tips or important notes**
> Appear like this.

Get in touch

Feedback from our readers is always welcome.

General feedback: If you have questions about any aspect of this book, email us at `customercare@packtpub.com` and mention the book title in the subject of your message.

Errata: Although we have taken every care to ensure the accuracy of our content, mistakes do happen. If you have found a mistake in this book, we would be grateful if you would report this to us. Please visit `www.packtpub.com/support/errata` and fill in the form.

Piracy: If you come across any illegal copies of our works in any form on the internet, we would be grateful if you would provide us with the location address or website name. Please contact us at `copyright@packt.com` with a link to the material.

If you are interested in becoming an author: If there is a topic that you have expertise in and you are interested in either writing or contributing to a book, please visit `authors.packtpub.com`.

Share Your Thoughts

Once you've read *Canva Cookbook*, we'd love to hear your thoughts! Scan the QR code below to go straight to the Amazon review page for this book and share your feedback.

https://packt.link/r/1-801-07530-1

Your review is important to us and the tech community and will help us make sure we're delivering excellent quality content.

Download a free PDF copy of this book

Thanks for purchasing this book!

Do you like to read on the go but are unable to carry your print books everywhere?

Is your eBook purchase not compatible with the device of your choice?

Don't worry, now with every Packt book you get a DRM-free PDF version of that book at no cost.

Read anywhere, any place, on any device. Search, copy, and paste code from your favorite technical books directly into your application.

The perks don't stop there, you can get exclusive access to discounts, newsletters, and great free content in your inbox daily

Follow these simple steps to get the benefits:

1. Scan the QR code or visit the link below

https://packt.link/free-ebook/9781801075305

2. Submit your proof of purchase
3. That's it! We'll send your free PDF and other benefits to your email directly

1

Introducing Canva
and Its Interface

Imagine turning your creative ideas into professional-looking visual content, even if you have no design experience. Sounds impossible, right? Wrong! That's the magic of Canva, a user-friendly design platform that democratizes graphic design for everyone.

I am Barbara, a professional designer and your Canva coach, and this first chapter serves as your gateway to the exciting world of Canva. Here, we'll delve into its core features, navigate the interface, and equip you with essential design principles.

Think of Canva as your portable design studio, accessible on your computer, tablet, or even phone. Sure, the interface might get a makeover every now and then (think of it as a fun fashion update!), but the core features remain the same.

In this chapter, we'll cover the following topics:

- Discovering Canva's main interfaces
- Incorporating external resources and reviewing Canva's limits
- Implementing useful shortcuts

Technical requirements

To follow along with this chapter – and the rest of the book – you will just need Canva.

Saying that, it's important to note that Canva has some features that require a paid subscription. But fear not, design grasshopper; we'll be exploring both the free and paid sides – so whether you're rocking a budget tighter than a drumhead or have pockets overflowing with digital doubloons, we've got you covered.

Discovering Canva's main interfaces

Though Canva is extremely user-friendly, it might seem like a magical land of visual delights, and you may need some help navigating around the different interfaces.

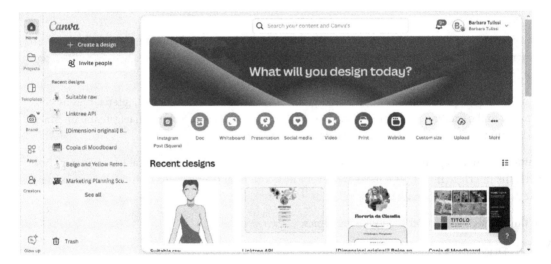

Figure 1.1: Canva's dashboard

So, let's demystify the Canva interface together and explore some of its different features.

Canva search bar

Feeling the blank page panic? Fear not, design friend! Ditch the template hunt, tell the search bar what you want, and POOF! Canva's magic AI whips up a unique design just for you!

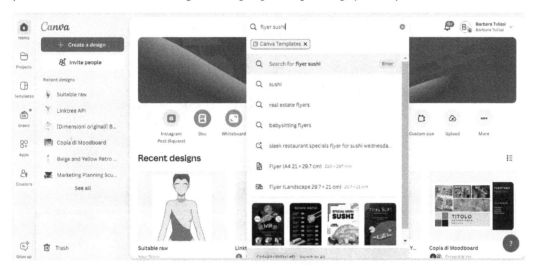

Figure 1.2: Canva's search bar

The search bar isn't just your keyword buddy anymore – it's a creative partner, understanding your ideas and generating designs based on your prompts. Think of it like ChatGPT for design.

But remember, our AI baby is still learning, so keep your prompts simple and concise. If you want to make an event about sushi, search for `sushi Wednesday` or `flyer sushi`. Adding a color to your prompt will also help you to find a template that suits your business, such as `green flyer sushi`.

Also, currently, the search bar only works in English (for now; more languages are coming soon!).

And another thing – even if you do not remember the name of a project, you can search for the style you gave it, the color codes used, or words featured in the design. Essentially, you can search for nearly anything you remember about the project and Canva should be able to find it for you!

Visual Suite

Since March 2023, Canva has transformed into a Visual Suite, serving up an array of eye-catching layouts right under your search bar. Need a social media post or a Pinterest pin? Easy peasy! Craving a video edit or a document template? You've got it! Invoices, estimates, mind maps, shopping lists, even CVs and presentations – Canva's your one-stop shop for all things visual.

Visual Suite

Figure 1.3: Canva's Visual Suite

All the design types have been grouped into macro-categories, so just click on the category you need and look for a specific premade template or a blank one.

Templates

Feeling uninspired and stuck staring at a blank canvas? Don't worry, you're not alone! That's where Canva templates come in. Instead of starting from scratch, you can use a template as a springboard, customizing it with your own colors, fonts, and images to make it unique.

And the best part? Even if you end up with something completely different from the template, it doesn't matter! The template just sparked your imagination and helped you get started.

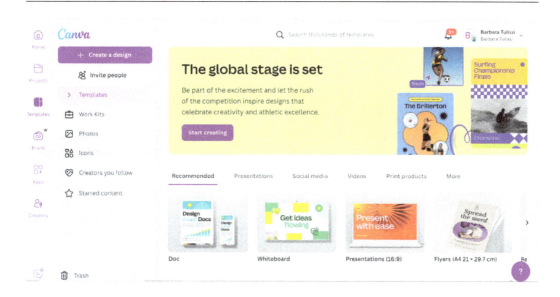

Figure 1.4: Templates page

Let's suppose we are looking for inspiration to design social content about interior design. Click the **Template** option on the left-hand toolbar and, from the search bar, enter the keyword you are looking for. We'll enter Interior design. Then, based on your color palette, let's assume you want to find a template for Instagram that is predominantly white. You can just open the template's filters, tick the **Instagram post** category, and select the color **White**. This way, you can find results that are closest to your needs without wasting time on uninteresting results.

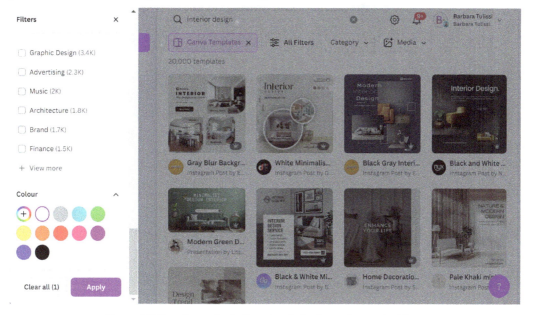

Figure 1.5: Search results for "interior design" templates, plus filters

Brand Hub

Brand element management can be cumbersome; however, if you have a Pro subscription, consider utilizing Canva's **Brand Hub** – this is your centralized storage space for all the logos, colors, fonts, and other assets of the brand (or *brands*) you may be managing. The Brand Hub eliminates the need for scattered folder structures and provides easy access in a single in-cloud location.

Even free users can leverage limited functionality by storing up to three essential brand colors. For extended functionality, consider creating a custom project (794x1,890 pixels) to serve as a DIY Brand Hub, housing logos, color codes, fonts, and relevant branding imagery, all saved in one handy document.

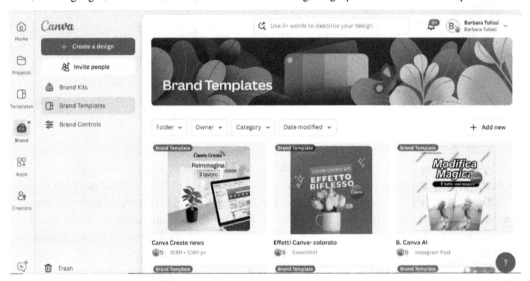

Figure 1.6: Brand Templates page

Alternatively, you can access a pre-made Brand Hub template (created by me!) here: https://partner.canva.com/eK5vY1. You can customize the template to suit your specific needs and populate it with relevant branding elements to establish a consistent and organized brand identity.

Figure 1.7: My pre-made Brand Hub template

Remember, effective organization enhances efficiency and streamlines design processes. Implement these suggestions to optimize your brand element management within Canva.

Plus, are you stuck with your brand voice? Canva Pro's got your back! Since October 2023, you can store your brand tone right in the Hub with its AI writing tool. Canva's AI brand voice feature is not just a text generator, though; it's a powerful tool for harnessing the magic of consistency and injecting personality into your brand communication.

Think of it as a whisper coach: you define your brand voice guidelines, including vocabulary, tone, and personality traits. The AI then analyzes these guidelines and learns your brand's "language." When you want to generate content, the AI will suggest text tailored to your specific voice. The AI doesn't simply parrot your existing content either – it uses its understanding of your brand to generate fresh, original text that aligns with your desired tone and message.

To find this feature, make sure that you're in the **Brand Hub** and scroll down until you find **Brand voice**. Then you can tell Canva how to generate text using the same tone your brand is using, such as `confident, casual, and friendly`.

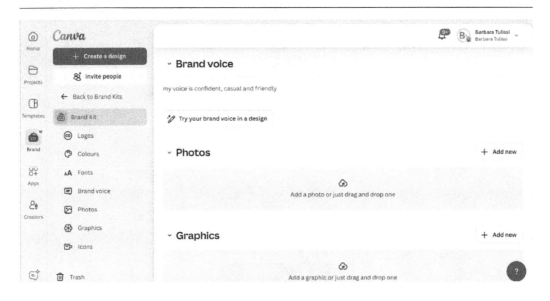

Figure 1.8: Canva's brand voice

To have a taste of how it sounds, click on **Try your brand voice in a design** and a new document will open up where you can write a prompt that will be used to generate a response in your set brand's voice:

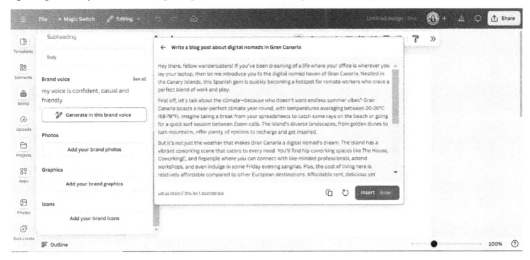

Figure 1.9: Canva's brand voice result

With this prompt, Canva's AI can help you with generating customized texts for your documents, posts, and presentations.

> **Note**
> Speaking of AI, Canva is packed with a whole host of AI features. In fact, we've dedicated *Chapter 11* to discussing them!

Single project interface

The single project page interface is our chameleon of Canva, changing and growing constantly, and is packed with features that we'll explore throughout the book!

Accessing design elements within Canva's project interface proves straightforward. Once you have a project option, as shown in *Figure 1.22*, navigate to the left toolbar menu. There are a few categories here, but the three main ones are **Elements**, **Text**, and **Uploads**:

- Need text? The **Text** section is here to help you add text boxes to your design.

- Got your own photos, videos, or audio? Upload them straight from your device using the **Uploads** section.

- Looking for something extra? The **Elements** section offers a wider range of design elements for you to choose from.

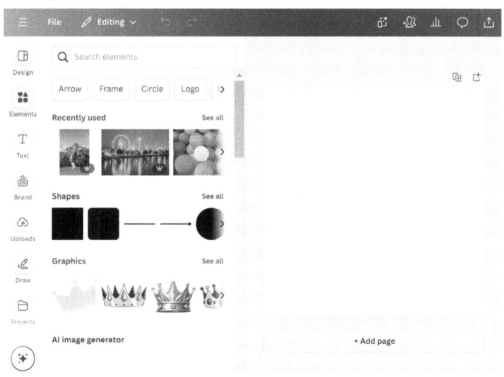

Figure 1.10: Single project interface

Looking at the **Elements** category specifically, it houses various design components, such as illustrations, icons, images, videos, shapes, grids, graphs, and layouts. These elements boast diverse origins, including contributions from creators like myself, enriching the available selection for Canva subscribers.

Furthermore, clicking the three dots (…) beside any element reveals the creator's name, additional information, and suggestions for similar elements. You can even follow creators directly within Canva, allowing convenient access to their future content.

Additionally, if you click on **Info**, you can also do the following:

- Mark the element as favorite: this will add the element to the favorite folder

- Add it to a specific folder of your choice

- Be redirected to similar elements

- See all the other related elements (if the element is part of a wider collection)

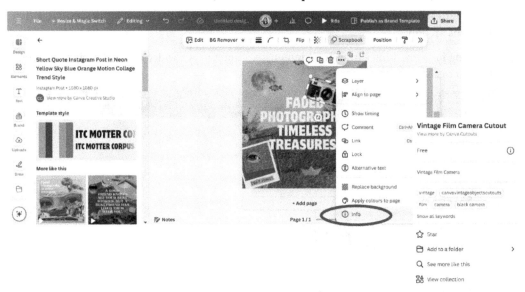

Figure 1.11: Magic recommendations and element creator details

However, be careful when using these elements. You cannot download an illustration and simply use it as a logo or icon just as it is; you will have to customize it with your own colors or use the illustration as part of a larger graphic. This way, Canva enforces copyright by protecting the work of its creators.

> **Note**
> You can find more information about Canva copyright here: `https://www.canva.com /help/licenses-copyright-legal-commercial-use/`.

Create a design button

Does your project canvas feel barren? Simply utilize the **Create a Design** button to initiate project creation.

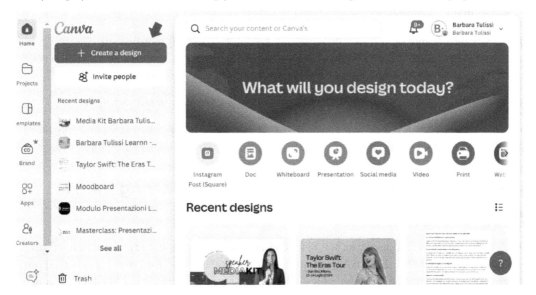

Figure 1.12: Create a design button

While the search bar aims to lead you through templates or projects by searching for keywords, the **Create a design** button allows you to directly find the type of design you want to create (for example, an Instagram story). This lets you bypass pre-defined templates and set custom dimensions, allowing you to unleash your design potential without restraint!

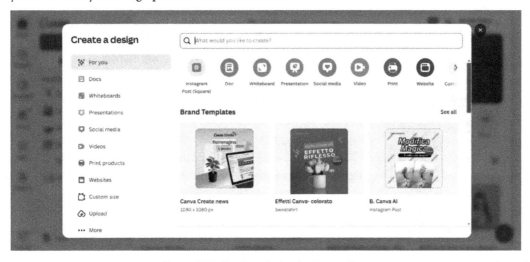

Figure 1.13: Create a design button options

On top of that, have you ever been stuck in a situation where you have a PDF and you can't copy the text? The **Create a design** button also lets you upload PDFs and make them completely editable. Some designers use this option to upload brand identities that were made in Adobe Illustrator but exported as PDFs.

Plus, the **Create a design** button lets you adjust images without opening a project too. This way, you do not need to download other photo editing apps to quickly adjust the colors or add a filter to your picture. It's your design pit stop for quick fixes and instant satisfaction.

After that overview of the main interfaces of Canva, one thing you may be wondering is

what you can upload in Canva. If so, stay with me. In the next section, I will give you some more details about the storage you can use in Canva and the upload limits.

Incorporating external resources and reviewing Canva limits

In Canva, the **Uploads** section allows you to upload external resources and save them in the Canva cloud space – for free users, this is 5 GB (on average, over 3,000 images); for Pro users, it is 1 TB (on average, over 600,000 images); and for education and non-profit accounts, it is 100 GB (on average, over 60,000 images).

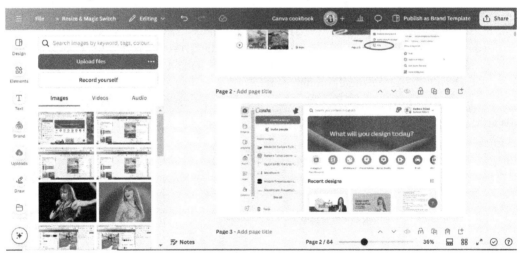

Figure 1.14: Canva's upload section

Even though I have hardly seen the storage space on Canva run out, I still advise you to upload images that are never larger than the design you are creating. For example, if you are creating an Instagram story measuring 1,080x1,920 pixels and you want to use a full-screen photo of yourself, make sure that the image is no larger than 1,920 pixels. If you instead were to create a 1x2 meter roll-up, you would need a larger image, at least 2 meters in size (i.e., 7,559 pixels), otherwise the previous 1,920px image would be grainy.

Figure 1.15: Low- and high-resolution images

Saying that, there are some upload limitations. In terms of the files, there is the following:

- The image file (.jpeg, .png, .svg) limit is 25 MB
- The audio file (.m4a, .mp3, etc.) limit is 250 MB
- The video file (.mov, .mp4, etc.) is 1 GB

And in terms of users, there is the following:

- The limit for free users is up to 1 GB
- There is no specific limit for Canva Pro/Teams users (it is likely just very big)

Let's also take a look at some of the supported file types. The supported image formats are as follows:

- .png and .jpg/jpeg: These are the most common image formats
- .heic: Most iPhone and iPad pictures are automatically saved in this format
- .svg: A vectorial format, mostly used for logos

While the supported video formats are as follows:

- .mov: This is Apple's video format
- .gif: Used for animated web images for the web, such as icons and short loops (memes!), but not for photos or long videos.
- .mp4: The widest multimedia container format
- .mpeg: A format that uses compression to make the file smaller
- .mkv: Good for high-quality videos with multiple language options
- .webm: A free, web-friendly video format designed for streaming

If you are wondering how you can find out the format, size, extent, or weight of the image from your PC, simply right-click the image and view the image properties:

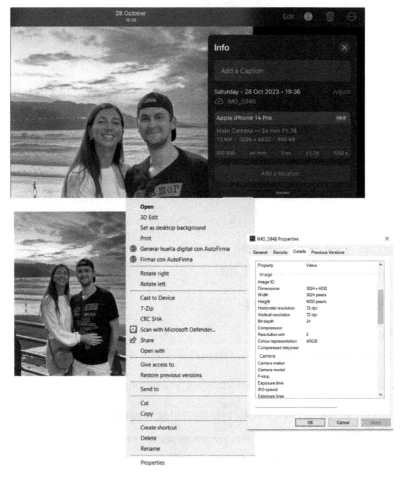

Figure 1.16: Image information on Mac (top) and Windows (bottom)

If you're using your phone, just find your image and open the image's information panel:

Figure 1.17: Image information on a phone (iPhone)

After that, if you need to change properties, you can use this powerful and free converter: `https://www.iloveimg.com/`.

Also, to quickly convert pixels into centimeters or other units of measurement, you can simply use the Google Converter: `https://cloudconvert.com/`.

> **Note**
>
> Before starting a project, it's worth remembering that the minimum size for your project is 40x40 pixels (1,058 x 1,058 cm), while the maximum is 8,000 x 3,125 pixels (211,664 x 82,681 cm).

After quickly reviewing the Upload section and some Canva limits, let's now quickly review some helpful shortcuts you should remember.

Implementing useful shortcuts

To speed up your work in Canva you can use a series of shortcuts from your desktop. Here are some of the Canva shortcuts that I use daily to speed up my work:

Function	Windows Shortcut	Mac Shortcut
Undo	Ctrl + Z	Command + Z
Select all	Ctrl + A	Command + A
Add text	T	T
Add rectangle	R	R
Add circle	C	C
Add line	L	L
Toggle rulers and guides	Shift + R	Shift + R

Figure 1.30: Shortcuts

Besides these, you can find other shortcuts here: https://www.canva.com/help/keyboard-shortcuts/.

Summary

Level up, designer – you have now finished the first chapter and unlocked some of Canva's essential features!

Throughout this chapter, we have navigated through Canva's interface, discovering the search bar (powered by AI!), its streamlined single project interface, and the multi-purpose **Create a design** button. Just for Pro users, we also met the Brand Hub; however, we looked at how Free users can still use this feature too.

As well as the main interfaces, we also reviewed incorporating resources in the **Uploads** section, some of our tool's limitations, and some handy shortcuts.

Remember, Canva evolves, but your potential soars. Use this knowledge to explore and unleash your inner design genius!

In the next chapter, let's dive into brand archetypes and discover your creative personality!

2
Creating Your Brand and Shaping It in Canva

Ever felt that pang of envy when you see a brand such as Coca-Cola or Spotify be instantly recognized by a single logo or jingle? What is their secret sauce? It's not just about catchy slogans or fancy logos (although those definitely help!), it's about having a distinct personality, carefully crafted and consistently expressed through something called brand guidelines.

Every successful brand has a beating heart – a set of core values, a clear mission, and something that makes it stand out from the crowd. This chapter will guide you on a journey of self-discovery, helping you to identify the essence of your brand and articulate it in a way that resonates with your audience.

Imagine your brand coming alive and speaking directly to you – what would it say? How would it sound? We'll help you craft a unique and engaging voice that reflects your brand's personality and connects with your ideal customers.

And let's not forget the visual magic! Similar to a beautifully designed website, your brand needs a consistent and eye-catching aesthetic. We'll explore defining your color palette, choosing fonts that sing, and selecting design elements that'll tell your brand story without a single word.

So, in this chapter, we will cover the following main topics:

- Creating your brand
- Choosing your brand archetype
- Developing your brand's visual identity in Canva

Creating your brand

"Everything is brand," says Philip Kotler in his book, *Principles of Marketing. "The brand is everything that a product or service represents for consumers."*

A strong brand is similar to an atmosphere that envelops and influences its consumers. It is not just about the visual elements or the verbal messaging; it is about the overall experience that the brand creates.

Let's think about the Earth's atmosphere: it is made up of multiple layers that cannot exist alone; they need to stay together. A brand works in the same way. It is made up of multiple elements such as the company's scope, vision, mission, and values, with each layer being the result of the previous one.

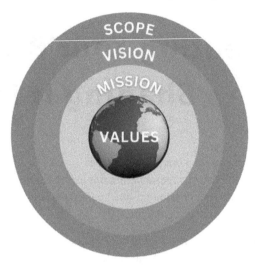

Figure 2.1: Brand atmosphere

Building a brand takes time, which is why I invite you to experience it as a challenge – more specifically, a four-day challenge. I recommend you do one section a day and, as you go on, you can review and modify the previous answers if necessary. In this challenge, it is important to let your ideas settle and evolve over time.

> **Note**
>
> In the following subsections, I have provided scope, vision, and mission statements from real companies; however, the statements themselves are made up, created by simply observing and studying these brands. You could always research your favorite company, or one in a similar area to your own brand, and try creating an appropriate scope, vision, and mission statement for it.
>
> Plus, we will follow a practical example. We will do this by imagining that we are social media managers interviewing Claudia, the owner of Claudia's Flowers, a new local shop, to understand her brand's core values and goals. With these sample answers, you should be able to reflect more deeply on your own brand too.
>
> When answering the questions, you can write on the lines provided (if you own the physical book), or use a separate notebook or digital document. This will not only give you more space to write your answers, but also let you tweak them over time.

Day 1: Scope

Your business' scope is your "forever", your North Star, and a source of inspiration and guidance that survives ups, downs, and changes. You should think of it as being about more than just profit – it's the underlying passion or mission that fuels the enterprise. This core purpose is often intangible, yet it's the bedrock upon which a business is built.

Here are some examples of business' scope:

- "Make people happy" – Disney
- "Experience the thrill of competition and victory" – Nike
- "Make the design something useful, not just beautiful" – my personal brand

To help find your scope, answer the following questions:

What drove you to create your brand (beyond the economic motivation)?

(*Claudia's Flowers*: "Driven by a lifelong love of nature and a talent for gardening, Claudia opened her shop to share her passion for plants. She finds joy in creating beautiful spaces and believes that surrounding oneself with greenery enhances one's well-being.")

What is the founding story of your company or personal brand? When did you decide to start this new adventure and why? What were your desires and fears?

(*Claudia's Flowers*: "Claudia has always had a deep connection to nature. Growing up in a small countryside town, she spent countless hours tending to her family's garden. As she grew older, her passion for plants blossomed into a desire to share her love for floral beauty with the world. After years of working in the corporate world, Claudia realized she needed a change. Inspired by the therapeutic nature of gardening and the joy it brought to others, she decided to turn her passion into a profession.")

Now try to condense the previous two answers together in a single idea – this will be your brand scope, your "forever"!

(*Claudia's Flowers*: "Enhancing lives through the transformative power of nature, one bloom at a time.")

Now let's take a closer look at your previous answers. Do they feel like they truly represent you and your brand? It's important to be honest with yourself here, but don't worry, it's not a test! Taking time for honest reflection can be valuable.

If you feel your answers don't quite capture your brand's essence, that's okay. Just take a break, let your ideas settle, and come back tomorrow to revise them. No pressure!

Day 2: Vision

The vision of your brand is your "one-day" idea, something that needs time and commitment to be accomplished. A vision allows you to establish an ideal to aim for, which will direct your daily actions.

To develop your vision, consider these questions:

If I perfectly execute everything I've dreamed of doing, how would people's lives be different? How would the world have changed?

To answer these, consider these two prompts:

1. "No [broad customer group here] will ever [problem/problems you are solving here]."
2. "All [broad customer group here] are able to [goal/goals of your vision here]."

Here are some useful examples of brand visions:

*   "No one will ever suffer from Alzheimer's disease" – Alzheimer's Association
*   "All people should be able to live in a decent place" – Habitat for Humanity
*   "No marketer will ever create ineffective designs" – my vision!

What about Claudia's Flowers? Their vision might be: "All people should be able to buy plants easily and enjoy the beauty of their flowers."

Now you can write your vision here:

_____

_____

_____

After that, take a day to review your answers in this exercise – reflect on how they match your brand voice and purpose. Then, refreshed and recharged, jump into the next day's exercise.

Day 3: Mission

If your vision is your "one day", then your mission is your "today," including all the actions you need to take daily to achieve your vision. While the vision is something abstract, the mission is something concrete.

Let's think of Claudia's vision. To achieve her vision of making floral beauty an accessible and essential part of everyone's life, Claudia should focus on the following daily actions:

- Prioritize customer satisfaction by understanding their needs, preferences, and occasions
- Ensure that the flowers and plants she sells are of the highest quality and freshness
- Continuously develop new and unique floral arrangements to inspire customers
- Build strong relationships with local businesses and residents through events, partnerships, and community involvement
- Implement sustainable, eco-friendly practices, such as sourcing local flowers and minimizing waste
- Share knowledge about plant care and floral design through workshops or social media
- Offer a variety of price points and product options to cater to different budgets and tastes

Now, what actions need to be taken on a daily basis to achieve your brand's purpose and vision?

- _____
- _____
- _____

Next, who are the people you'd most like to engage with your brand through the products/services you offer?

Claudia wants to target individuals and businesses seeking to enhance their environment with the beauty of flowers. This could include the following:

- Individuals purchasing flowers for personal enjoyment, to be given as gifts, or to be used as home decor
- Businesses and organizations requiring floral arrangements for events, to be used as office decor, or given to clients as gifts
- Event planners organizing weddings, parties, and other events that need floral arrangements

What about your brand? Who is it aimed at?

- _____
- _____
- _____

How does your brand deliver value based on your customer's needs?

For example, Claudia's Flowers want to deliver value to customers by doing the following:

- Offering products that promote mental and emotional well-being through the beauty and tranquility of nature
- Creating customized floral arrangements to meet individual tastes and preferences, making customers feel special and valued
- Providing expert knowledge and guidance on floral care, design, and selection
- Offering a variety of purchasing options, including in-store, online, and delivery services for customer convenience
- Creating memorable experiences through events, workshops, and community engagement
- Prioritizing sustainable practices to align with customers' values and contribute to environmental well-being

You can fill out your answers here:

* _____
* _____
* _____

Finally, how is your approach unique compared to that of your competitors?

(*Claudia's Flowers*: "Claudia's Flowers' team offers a unique blend of nature, personalization, and community. We're not just florists; we're also storytellers, educators, and environmental stewards. Our commitment to sustainable practices and deep connection to nature is reflected in every arrangement.")

_____

_____

Now it's time to put all of these answers together! You can write your mission statement in different ways, but here I'll show you two methods and you can pick the one you prefer:

* "To offer [the goods or services you're offering] to [the people you are addressing] so that [the benefits these people will get]."
* "[Write one or more infinitive verbs that reflect the purpose of your brand + write down the people you are addressing] by [write your offer of goods or services] so that [write the benefits these people will get]."

Of course, you can omit one or more parts of this format to make your sentence work or be catchier on your website. Here are some useful examples to help you further:

* "Prevent and alleviate the suffering of those in an emergency situation, by mobilizing the power of volunteers and the generosity of donors, so that no one will ever suffer" – American Red Cross. (Structure used: brand's purpose + target audience + main offer + problem to be solved/benefit people get.)
* "Inspire and innovate every athlete in the world to live out their sporting dreams" – Nike. (Structure used: brand's purpose + target audience + benefit people get.)
* "Organize the world's information for all so that it is universally accessible" – Google. (Structure used: main offer + target audience + benefit people get.)

The mission statement for Claudia's Flowers might be: "To offer unique and personalized floral arrangements to individuals and businesses seeking to enhance their spaces and well-being, so that they can experience the transformative power of nature and create lasting memories."

You can write your mission statement here:

_____

_____

_____

Once you have your phrase, keep it safe – that phrase is the compass that will guide your actions every day!

High five for completing the challenge! Remember, even superheroes rest. Take 24 hours to refine your answers, aligning them with your brand's vision. Then, with renewed focus, you can move on to the next task!

Day 4: Values

Your brand values define the culture of your brand and how it operates. Values constitute your "now" because they are the principles that guide daily decisions as they occur, and they also dictate your behavior, particularly when things get tough. To work out what your values are, answer these questions:

What behaviors are important and non-negotiable, regardless of what you are doing?

* _____

* _____

* _____

The values for Claudia's Flowers include the following:

* A passion for nature – this is ultimately the heart of the brand and should be evident in everything the business does

* Building strong relationships with customers is essential for long-term success

* Continuously evolving and surprising customers with new and exciting floral designs

How do you embody your brand's mission in your day-to-day operations and interactions?

(*Claudia's Flowers*: "Claudia's Flowers thrives on a delicate balance of human connection, artistic flair, and environmental consciousness. By placing customers at the heart of her business model, and fostering genuine relationships with them, Claudia creates a loyal following. Her innate creativity drives innovation, ensuring the shop remains a vibrant and inspiring presence. Moreover, a deep-rooted respect for nature guides every decision, from sourcing to display, solidifying the brand's commitment to sustainability and ethical practices.")

_____

_____

_____

How would you describe yourself and your team (if you have one) when you are on top form?

(*Claudia's Flowers*: "I [Claudia] would describe myself and my team as passionate floral artisans. We are a harmonious blend of creativity and precision, dedicated to transforming spaces and emotions through our work. Our team is a living tapestry of talent, each thread contributing to the vibrant masterpiece that is Claudia's Flowers.")

_____

_____

_____

You will now see three tables – "Basic Values," "Extreme Values," and "Self-Actualization Values" – each containing a variety of core value keywords:

Basic Values:

Security	Trust	Health	Expertise
Compassion	Optimism	Curiosity	Hope

Extreme Values:

Honesty	Justice	Fairness	Efficiency
Progress	Love	Fun	Agility
Respect	Vision	Courage	Ecology
Gratitude	Emancipation	Equilibrium	Utility
Altruism	Generosity	Freedom	Tradition

Self-Actualization Values:

Leadership	Creativity	Integrity	Ethics
Prosperity	Individuality	Teamwork	Patience
Perseverance	Independence	Reliability	Empathy
Punctuality	Professionalism	Prestige	Responsibility

From each of the previous tables, choose between 1 and 3 core values and add them to the following table. Then, for each core value, explain what it means to you:

Core value	What it means to you

Here is what the table for Claudia's Flowers might look like:

Core value	What it means to you
Health	This value manifests in the shop's commitment to providing fresh, high-quality flowers that contribute to customers' well-being. It also extends to employee wellness, in an effort to provide a healthy work environment.
Gratitude	A culture of gratitude is fostered, recognizing the contributions of employees, customers, and suppliers. This positive atmosphere enhances teamwork and customer satisfaction.
Creativity	This value is at the heart of the business, driving innovation in floral design and ensuring that every arrangement is unique and inspiring.
Teamwork	Collaboration and mutual support are essential to the success of Claudia's Flowers. The team works harmoniously to achieve common goals.

Congratulations! You've braved the past four days, delving deep and laying the groundwork for a truly authentic brand identity. But before we rush headfirst into the next topic, allow yourself a well-deserved break. Take a 24-hour breather to revisit your answers. Read them critically, not just for clarity, but for honesty. Do they truly reflect your brand's heart and soul? Do they align with the image you want to project and the connection you hope to forge with your audience? Be your own toughest critic. Revise, refine, and ensure that every answer rings true.

Remember, authenticity is the cornerstone of any successful brand. Don't shy away from difficult truths or paint a picture that doesn't resonate with your core values. This honesty will form the foundation of your brand personality, allowing you to connect with your audience on a deeper, more meaningful level.

> **Tip**
>
> If you are building a personal brand, I also recommend you take the Jung test. This isn't one of those fun "What fruit are you?" tests, but a psychological test designed to categorize behavioral and psychological patterns and help you better understand who you are.
>
> To take the test, use this link: `https://www.16personalities.com/free-personality-test`.
>
> When you receive the result, read it very carefully and note down what attributes of your personality you want to incorporate into your brand communication and those that you don't.

The next part of this chapter contains an exciting exploration of brand archetypes. We'll discover what personality your brand embodies, whether it's the nurturing caregiver, the wise sage, or the daring outlaw. Through this lens, you'll gain invaluable insights into how to communicate with your audience in a way that resonates with their deepest desires and aspirations.

Creating a brand archetype

Imagine the stories you love. They usually involve a brave hero, a wise mentor, and a fun-loving trickster. These characters aren't just words on a page; they tap into something deeper in our minds. These powerful patterns are called archetypes. Think of them like mental shortcuts; instead of explaining every detail, they instantly conjure up feelings and ideas. No wonder they're powerful tools for brands!

Now picture your favorite company: does it feel friendly and relatable? Powerful and inspiring? That's the magic of archetypes – they connect with our core desires and values. So the next time you see a brand you love, ask yourself: what archetype do they fit into?

Crafting a strong brand can feel like a juggling act, but identifying your brand's archetype helps in two ways:

- Archetypes can help you find your communication style. Think of your brand's unique personality. Is it quirky and funny, similar to a jester, or reassuring and helpful, similar to a caregiver? The visual design and messaging should work together to communicate your message.

- Archetypes are universal characters that resonate with different audiences. By understanding which one (or ones) appeals to your customers (explorers, creators, etc.), you can tailor your message to better connect to your customers and gain their trust. Remember, it's about their interests, not yours.

> **Note**
>
> It's important to remember that you're basing your brand archetype on the characteristics of your business, not your ideal customer – this should be the primary archetype. However, choosing a secondary, complementary archetype based on your customers' needs will also help your business grow.

Take a look at *Figure 2.2* – it illustrates character archetypes; however, they can easily be adapted into brand archetypes, which can be used to craft your brand's personality:

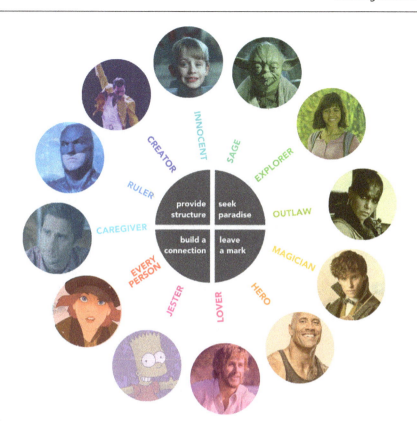

Figure 2.2: Character/brand archetypes

You can also see a further breakdown of the brand archetypes in the following table:

Character/ brand archetype	Main value	Personality attributes	Its color palette could be...	Brand examples
Creator	Innovation	Creativity. Imagination. Nonlinear thought. Nonconformity. Developed aesthetic.	Orange, red, dark gray, or black	Adobe, Apple, LEGO, and YouTube
Innocent	Safety	Unbridled sense of wonder. Purity. Freedom from preconceptions. Trust. Unconditional love. Spontaneity. Honesty. Wholesomeness	Blue, white, or yellow	Dove, Disney, Coca-Cola, and Aveeno

Character/ brand archetype	Main value	Personality attributes	Its color palette could be...	Brand examples
Sage	Wisdom	Wisdom. Intelligence. Truth-seeking. Clarity of thought. Rational decision-making. Prudence. Talent as a diligent researcher.	Blue, green, black, or dark gray	Wikipedia, Google, Discovery, and CNN
Explorer	Freedom	Independence. Bravery. Freedom. Self-sufficiency. Nonconformity.	Red, yellow, or green	National Geographic, Land Rover, and Airbnb
Outlaw	Liberation	Leadership. Risk taking. Progressive and provocative thought. Bravery. Personal power. Brutal honesty. Experimentation.	Orange, red, or yellow	Harley-Davidson, Crooked, Virgin, and Impossible
Magician	Power	Ability to dream enormous dreams. Mysterious powers of perception. Awe-inspiring intuition and cleverness. Charisma. Highly evolved perspective.	Red, white, black, or dark gray	Nintendo, TED, Dyson, and Tesla
Hero	Mastery	Self-sacrifice. Courage. Redemption. Transformation. Faith. Strength. Stamina.	Orange, yellow, black, or dark gray	Patagonia, Nike, and Gatorade
Lover	Intimacy	Faithfulness. Passionate sensuality, sexuality, and spirituality. Expansiveness. Vitality. Appreciation.	Gold, red, or pink	Godiva, Chanel, and Victoria's Secret
Jester	Enjoyment	Wicked humor. Originality. Irreverence. Present moment awareness. Facile social skills.	Orange, red, or yellow	Skittles, KFC, and Burger King
Everyperson	Belonging	Stewardship. Altruism. Respect. Fairness. Accountability. Tendency to be a good listener and hard worker.	Blue, red, or brown/tan	IKEA, Levi's, and The Home Depot

Character/ brand archetype	Main value	Personality attributes	Its color palette could be...	Brand examples
Caregiver	Service	Altruism. Compassion. Patience. Empathy.	Blue, white, or turquoise	Volvo, Toms, Johnson & Johnson, and Marriott International
Ruler	Control	Power. Confidence. Dominion. High Status. Leadership.	Gold, silver, or black	Rolex, Louis Vuitton, and Mercedes-Benz

Table 2.3: Character/brand archetype breakdown

Now based on the previous information, try to follow these easy steps to find your brand archetype(s):

1. Look at *Figure 2.2*. Based on pure instinct, which archetype do you think reflects your brand best? Does it better fit the Creator or Explorer archetype? I think mine is more aligned with the Explorer archetype.

2. Now look at *Figure 2.3*. After seeing the breakdown of the archetypes, do you now have a different answer for which archetype reflects your brand best? My first instinct was that my brand fit the Explorer archetype, but after reading about the Creator archetype, I think it fits that archetype more.

3. Take another look at *Figure 2.3*. Is there a second archetype that fits your brand, particularly one that is relevant and complementary to the relationship you want to build with your customers? Personally, I know my audience wants to leave a mark by learning how to improve their design skills, so I think my second archetype is the Magician archetype.

Once you have answered these questions, you should have a better idea of what your brand archetype is.

While this chapter has explored brand guidelines and archetypes from a theoretical perspective, the journey doesn't end here. The next section will equip you with the knowledge to transform these concepts into action using Canva, reviewing the powerful tool that will help you bring your brand vision to life.

Developing your brand visual identity in Canva

Feeling overwhelmed by the visual side of branding? This section is your cheat sheet for developing your brand's visual identity in Canva. We'll ditch the jargon and get straight to the good stuff: crafting mood boards that capture your vision, picking color palettes that pop, and choosing fonts that speak your brand's language. We'll have your brand looking sharper than ever, without the need for any in-depth design knowledge. Let's turn your brand into a visual masterpiece, one click at a time!

Mood board

Your graphics style should be as unique as your fingerprint. Just as Van Gogh's work couldn't be mistaken for Picasso's, and vice versa, your brand should have unique, immediately recognizable visuals.

A brand mood board is perhaps one of the most subjective parts of the entire design process, as it aims to encompass all your sources of inspiration. Imagine it as a large blank canvas on which you can draw, doodle, glue, and post whatever you want without rules.

Start by reflecting on your brand's core values and personality. What vibe do you want to evoke? What feelings should your graphics inspire? Then gather imagery that resonates with your vision. Experiment with different approaches but stay true to your brand's essence. From your mood board, you should be able to do the following:

- See the brand's color palette, which should be a harmonic combination of colors that represent your brand
- Identify the brand's fonts and font hierarchy
- Describe the brand's visual communication style

To create a mood board, you can use the Canva template that I have prepared for you: `https://partner.canva.com/PyXEqQ`

Alternatively, go to Canva's **Template** page and search for `mood board`, `vision board`, or just `whiteboard` if you prefer to start from a blank page.

Then, from the **Elements** section of Canva, drop anything you want into your mood board, such as images, videos, illustrations, shapes, and textures.

Figure 2.4: Example of a mood board

I also find Pinterest very useful, as it contains many examples of and ideas for Canva mood boards as well as visuals you can include in your mood boards. When you find an interesting visual reference on Pinterest, you can download it and upload it to Canva, ready to add to your board.

Elements

As mentioned, to create a mood board, you can use a pre-made template; however, I prefer to open a blank project and add a lot of elements, images, stickers, and so on, without any logic. Ultimately, it's a subjective process, and I need to unleash all the inspiration and ideas I have in my mind.

To make it easier for you, especially if you are not used to this process, let's fill our mood board with just three images, elements, or videos that resonate with you and embody your brand's core values. To help you do this, I recommend writing down your brand's top three values on your mood board. They'll be there as a reminder throughout the process.

Then, jump into Canva and explore the **Elements** option. Here you can navigate through shapes, graphics, stickers, images, videos, and much more. Search for visuals using keywords related to your brand. For example, the owner of a flower shop might search for `flowers`. But don't limit yourself to your niche! The key is to find visuals that spark a connection with your brand values, even if they seem unrelated at first glance. As you browse, keep asking yourself this critical question: "Does this image truly represent at least one of my brand's values?" This question will be your guidepost for making all your mood board choices.

Color

Once you have added all the assets you want to your mood board, I recommend moving on to choosing the brand's colors. In the mood board template I provided, use the four circles on the top right. If you're creating your own mood board, you can add your own circles and color them to represent your brand colors.

To fill the circles with color, click one of them, and an editing menu will show at the top. Here, select the **Colour** box. Within the **Colour** panel, you'll find four main sections:

- **Document colours**: These are the colors that are currently used on shapes/fonts in the document/project you are working on.
- **Brand kit colours**: If you are using Canva Pro, you will find your palette here (we will discuss brand kits in more detail shortly).

- **Photo colours**: When you add an image to your design, Canva cleverly detects the most prominent colors used within it. These detected colors are then displayed here, offering you a convenient way to incorporate the image's color palette into your broader design.

- **Default colours**: This section offers a selection of pre-defined colors and gradients for you to choose from.

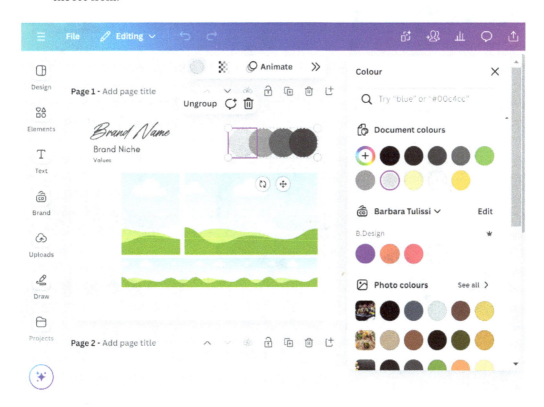

Figure 2.5: The Colour menu

If there is a color present in an element of your mood board, and it wasn't automatically picked up in the **Photo colours** section, you can always extract it directly from the image. To do this, simply click on the + icon enclosed in the rainbow-colored circle under **Document colours** (the first circle icon), then click on the dropper icon. Once the dropper tool is activated, select the desired color from the element/image:

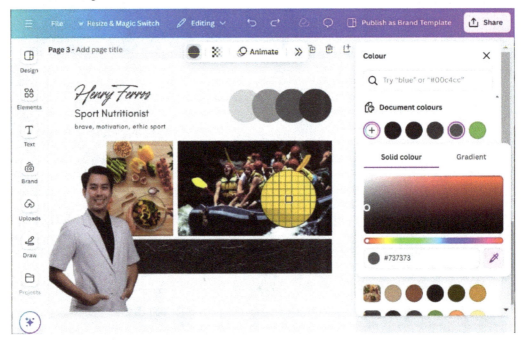

Figure 2.6: The color picker option

When creating your palette, try to select the colors that reflect your brand's identity best. Your color palette should be made up of 3 to 5 colors, of which two should be white and black. By "white" and "black," I do not mean solid black and white, but colors that are light enough and dark enough to be considered neutral. So, once the first circle has been filled, repeat the operation up to four more times.

Now look at your palette. What feeling does it give you? Do you think it could represent your brand's values? Are the colors too dark or too light? Is there something out of place? Are some color combinations too strong? Based on your answers you will replace or modify the colors. If you want to manually adjust the tint or shade of a particular color within Canva, you can always click on the + icon in the **Colour** panel:

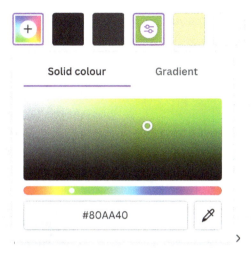

Figure 2.7: Customizing your colors

Finally, I want to give you two free tools that you can use to find your color palette and to learn more about color theory:

- **Color Palette Generator** (`https://www.canva.com/colors/color-palette-generator/`) is a free Canva tool that allows you to obtain a color palette from an image or search by keyword. For example, by searching for `ocean`, I can find ocean-themed palettes, or by searching for `purple`, I can find palettes where purple is harmoniously combined with other colors.

Color palettes

Figure 2.8: The Color Palette Generator website

- **Color wheel** (`https://www.canva.com/colors/color-wheel/`) is a Canva tool that allows you to create a palette according to color theory using the wheel. I usually recommend this tool to professional designers.

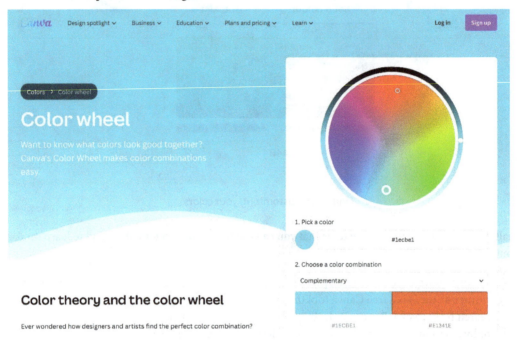

Figure 2.9: Canva's color wheel

Fonts

Now you want to choose the right fonts. Ultimately, your chosen font should have a single characteristic: it must be *readable*. Text in an illegible font risks not being read, preventing your message from being communicated effectively.

When creating a mood board, always choose a maximum of three fonts. Why three, you may ask? Well, imagine your design has a voice. While you want its voice to be unique, introducing too many fonts can make it difficult to understand. Sticking to three fonts ensures clarity, allowing the message to be delivered to the viewer clearly without overwhelming them.

Do not struggle with font combinations! You can take inspiration from the font combos you already find on Canva under the **Text** options.

Figure 2.10: Font combo section

When it comes to choosing your three fonts, they should each serve a purpose. Similar to a well-structured blog post, choosing the right fonts involves creating a visual hierarchy that guides the viewer's eye and emphasizes key information:

- First comes your title – it needs to be attention-grabbing, utilizing a bold, impactful font to draw viewers in and spark curiosity. This might be a decorative, display font that stands out visually.

- Next comes the subtitle, where you explain your main point. Here, you shift to a slightly smaller, yet clear and readable, font that complements the title.

- Finally, the text serves as the body of your conversation, offering details and explanations, as well as the core message. The font size used for text should be the smallest of the three, how it should still be comfortable to read even at a glance, clean, and visually similar to the other two fonts.

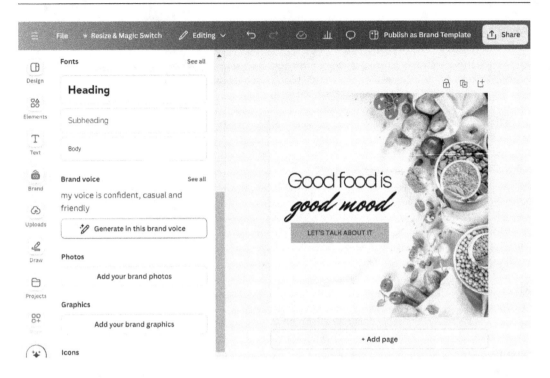

Figure 2.11: Font hierarchy

Also, always remember to keep your brand and mood board in mind when choosing the fonts. For example, look at the following two fonts. What niche does the first font belong to – gaming or beauty? What about the second?

Figure 2.12: Choosing fonts based on your brand

As you move forward, always remember to reflect and ask yourself: are these fonts in harmony with the color palette I've created? Do they express my brand values?

Icons, images, and illustrations

At this point, you may want to add icons or illustrations that represent your brand. However, remember that it is important that they have the same style.

Let's play a game. Which icons do you think have the same style?

Figure 2.13: Icon quiz

Answers

1 = c, 2 = d, 3 = b, 4 = e, 5 = a

Throw out the rulebook, you say? Well, experimenting with different styles for your icons can be tempting. But hold on – there's a strategic reason why brands keep them consistent. Think of your icons and illustrations as your squad. If they all have wildly different styles, it's hard to recognize them as a cohesive unit.

Maintaining a consistent design helps users instantly identify your brand across different platforms, similar to you recognizing your bestie in a crowd. This strengthens your brand identity, making it easier for people to remember you and connect with your message across the social media landscape.

So, while a little creative exploration is always welcome, remember that a unified look goes a long way in building a strong and recognizable online presence.

Now, is your mood board ready? Step back and take a critical look. Does it truly sing your brand's song? If not, refine it until it does! Remember, finding your perfect style takes time and exploration, so keep creating, keep experimenting, and let your unique visual voice shine through!

Brand Hub

Once you have all your brand assets set, you can create brand kits and efficiently manage them by utilizing Canva's Brand Hub (a Canva Pro feature). This platform allows you to centralize your colors, fonts, logos, and other brand assets, ensuring consistency across all your marketing materials.

You can access Brand Hub by clicking **Brand** on your Canva dashboard. On the left, you can see the following three options:

- In **Brand Kits**, you can create and view multiple brand kits:

Figure 2.14: Finding a brand kit from the Canva dashboard

- In **Brand Templates**, you can store design templates that you can use to quickly create specific brand-related projects:

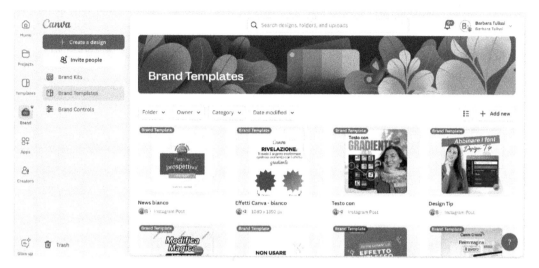

Figure 2.15: Brand Templates section

- In **Brand Controls**, you can control team access to brand assets:

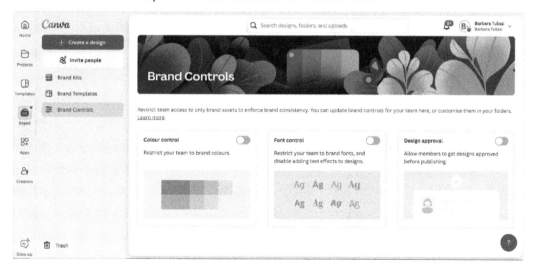

Figure 2.16: The Brand Controls section

Now, in **Brand Kits**, click + **Add new** to create a brand kit. By doing so, you can do the following:

- Upload your brand logo in all its glory (the .svg format is best because it won't pixelate the logo no matter where you put it – it is a vector file format!):

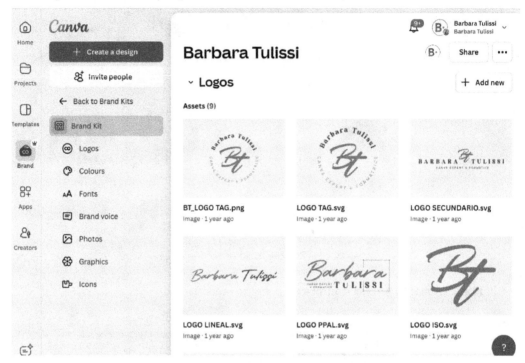

Figure 2.17: Exploring the Brand Kit feature

> **Note**
> Those using the free version of Canva cannot upload a logo.

- Upload your custom fonts:

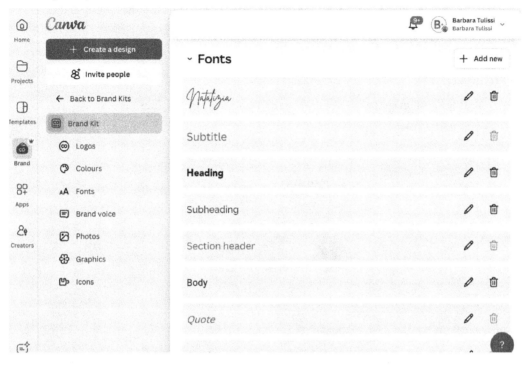

Figure 2.18: The Fonts section in Canva's Brand Kit

Note

Those using the free version of Canva can still find similar free fonts.

- Copy and paste your color's hex codes (similar to magic spells!) into Canva's Brand Hub or your brand identity template for quick access later. Remember, Canva uses hex, RGB, and CMYK systems, which are color code systems:

  - Hexadecimal for digital displays (short alphanumeric code such as #ffff)

  - RGB (red, green, and blue) for mixing colored lights

  - CMYK (cyan, magenta, yellow, and black) for mixing printing inks

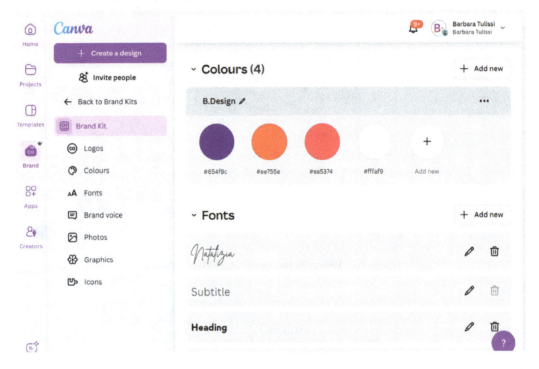

Figure 2.19: Color palette in Canva's Brand Kit

> **Note**
>
> If you are using a free version of Canva, be aware that with the Brand Kit feature, you can only add up to three colors, while with the Pro subscription, you can add as many as you need.

- Store your brand's images, graphics, and icons, and set your tone of voice through a prompt so that you can effortlessly use them in all your marketing materials:

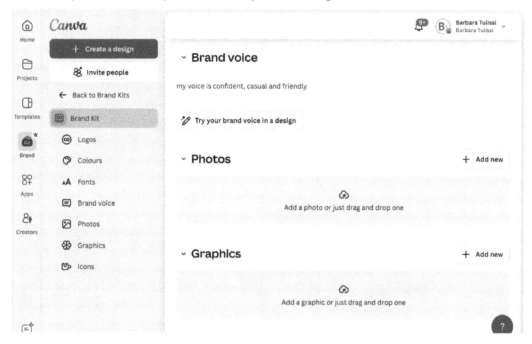

Figure 2.20: The Photos and Graphics sections in Canva's Brand Kit

Now that you have set up your brand kit, you are ready to dive further into the creative process.

Summary

This chapter wasn't just conveying information, it was also a brand-building launchpad!

In this chapter, we explored your brand's core vision, mission, and values, defining the unique "why" that will inform each of your branding decisions. We also unlocked the secret sauce of audience connection – identifying your brand archetype – and created a visual feast, your mood board, which ensures that your brand has a consistent visual identity.

Why is this exciting? Because a strong brand, similar to a rocket taking off, attracts the right customers, fosters their fierce loyalty, and blasts you past the competition!

Now, equipped with these initial building blocks, you're ready to shape a brand as unique and memorable as you are and start getting hands-on with Canva. Remember, consistency is your fuel, so keep it rolling!

3
Personalizing Your Social Media Presence

Hey there, content creators, social media managers, and designers—basically anyone who wants their social media presence to pop! Ever scrolled through your feed and seen a person's account that just screams "them"? Yeah, that's the power of social media personalization. It's all about crafting a visual identity that reflects your unique style and brand.

This chapter is your roadmap to mastering social personalization with Canva. We'll dive into creating a visually appealing social media strategy, but remember, one size doesn't fit all! Each platform has its own quirks and dimensions, so we'll cover recipes specifically tailored to popular platforms such as Instagram and Facebook.

I highly recommend checking out the first section, as it will lay the groundwork for creating a cohesive social skin across all your channels, but after that feel free to jump ahead to the platform you use most.

Also, remember—have fun with the design process! Keep your mood board and brand identity close at hand, and let's get your social media looking its best.

In this chapter, we will cover the following recipes:

- Crafting your brand's tone of voice
- Improving your profile picture
- Creating an Instagram grid mockup
- Designing social covers for Facebook, LinkedIn, and YouTube

Crafting your brand's tone of voice

Your tone of voice isn't just related to how you speak – it relates to your entire communication style, including through text and visuals. Think of it as your unique fingerprint on social media. It's how you connect with your audience and make them feel something.

Take the brands Coca-Cola and Oatly as examples. Don't they instantly conjure up different personalities? Coca-Cola is bold and energetic, while Oatly is friendly and down to earth. Their voice—in both the text and the visuals—reflects that perfectly.

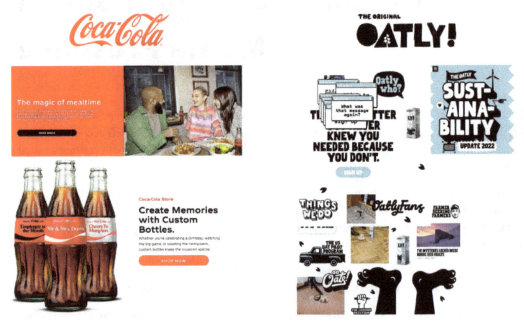

Figure 3.1: Coca-Cola and Oatly's tone of voice

The social media landscape is crowded, with everyone vying for attention, but with a strong tone of voice, you can rise above the noise and make your brand truly unforgettable.

This recipe is your guide to finding your brand's voice. Before getting deeper into Canva creation, I think it's important for you to define your tone of voice, so you will be able to craft incredible content that resonates better with your personal or company brand identity.

Getting ready

Before defining your tone of voice, I suggest you complete the exercises in *Chapter 2* to deeply know what your personal or company brand aims to communicate (its vision, mission, and values). Once done, you can continue with this recipe.

How to do it...

Defining your brand's tone of voice is akin to crafting a unique personality. While your personal style undoubtedly influences this process, remember that your brand is a distinct entity with its own character. By aligning your brand's voice with your target audience's preferences, you can build a connection that fosters loyalty and trust.

It's hard to get an idea of a tone of voice though. Try out this task to help with this:

1. Imagine your business is a person—do they have a specific gender? What do they look like? What are they wearing?

2. Now imagine their attitude—how do they behave? Are they friendly or cold? Funny or serious?

3. Complete these two sentences to help find a clear idea of your tone of voice:

   - "He is / she is / they are / it is …"

     For example: "He is a relatable young adult who wears T-shirts and shorts, and many hats—literally and figuratively. He is a total goofball, cracking jokes and lightening the mood. But when it comes to his area of expertise, he transforms into a serious, knowledgeable voice, someone you can trust for insightful advice. Imagine your favorite encouraging friend who can also get down to business, always offering a listening ear and words of encouragement!"

   - "He is / she is / they are / it is *not*…"

     For example: "He is not formally dressed, does not mock people or discourage people while learning new things, and does not put pressure on his friends and community."

4. Take a step back from this exercise—go out, sleep, do yoga, or do whatever you normally do to unwind to temporarily forget this exercise—then come back later or tomorrow. With time and space, you will be able to think about and improve your answers/tone of voice further.

Now that you've defined your tone of voice, you're ready to tackle the exercise that every brand does once it's defined its tone of voice. Take a look at the following table. For each tone, assign a score from 1 (not at all) to 5 (completely). This will help you visualize your brand voice and understand the overall tone you want to convey when communicating with your audience.

	1	2	3	4	5	
Formal						Informal
Hilarious						Earnest
Respectful						Irreverent
Enthusiastic						Practical

Ah, the beauty of a multi-faceted voice! Your brand's voice can have all sorts of tones, and that's a good thing. It allows you to be truly unique and stand out from the crowd.

Now, how do you translate that voice into your designs? With a little practice and this handy checklist, you can bridge the gap between your brand's voice and its visual identity. Think of this checklist as your secret weapon:

- Do the fonts, colors, and image styles you've chosen work together to express your desired tone? Is it a cohesive and visually appealing representation of your brand's voice?

- Does your design feel like a copycat of something you've seen elsewhere? Remember, you want to be original and grab attention!

- Are the design elements singing in harmony with your overall brand identity? Fonts, colors, and image styles should all tell the same story and reflect your brand's core voice.

- Does your design visually communicate the message you want to convey with your words? Is there a clear connection between the visuals and the tone expressed in your text?

Before hitting publish on your design, take a good look at it through the lens of this checklist. Mastering your brand voice is a surefire way to elevate your social media graphics and make them shine brighter than the competition. So go forth, experiment, have fun, and let your brand's unique voice be seen and heard!

> **Note**
>
> For companies with established brands, things might be a little different. The brand book, your company's style bible, probably already outlines a tone of voice. But what if your manager or client wants to shake things up a bit on social media?
>
> Here's my secret weapon: even in a corporate setting, a friendly and warm approach often wins on social media. It fosters connection and builds rapport with your audience, making your content more engaging and memorable.

Improving your profile picture

Your profile picture is like a tiny billboard for you or your brand. It's the first thing people see, so you want it to make a great first impression!

In this recipe, I will help you create a profile picture that's clear, reflects your personality, and makes you stand out. More specifically, we will improve a profile picture using a part-transparent circle method, which will help you get a clearer idea of how your profile picture will appear on your social media.

> **Note for businesses**
>
> Uploading your logo is an option, but only if it's clear and legible at a small size. Ideally, your designer should have provided a round version specifically designed for social media profiles.

How to do it...

To improve your profile image, take the following steps:

1. Open a project measuring 1,080x1,080 px (the same format as an Instagram post).
2. Upload your photo to Canva's **Uploads** section and insert the image into your design.
3. Next, we want to remove the background of the photo:

    *   If you have Canva Pro, you can do this by using **BG Remover** by clicking on the image and then the **Edit photo** option.
    *   If you are using the free version of Canva, you can go to `remove.bg`, which does the same thing.

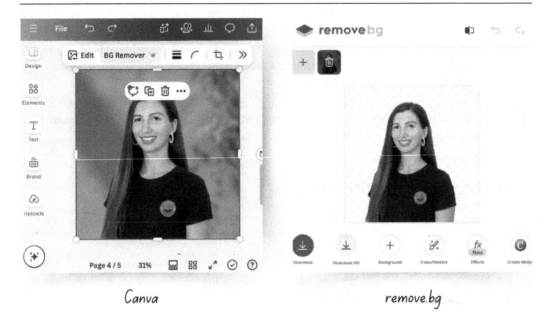

Figure 3.2: Removing a photo's background with Canva Pro and remove.bg

4. Once you have removed the background, go to **Edit** and search for the **Shadows** option. From there, choose **Outline** and alter the size and color of the shadow as desired (for the color, I have chosen purple).

Figure 3.3: Creating an outline using shadows

5. Now click on the area that was previously filled by the background image. You can then fill this area with a color, gradient, or a new image.

6. To get an accurate preview of how the profile image will look once uploaded onto your social media, press *C* on your keyboard to create a circle. Then extend it across the entire page.

7.   Color the circle black and lower the transparency to **10** to get an idea of the area that can be used for your profile image. Move your profile picture to make it fit into the circled area.

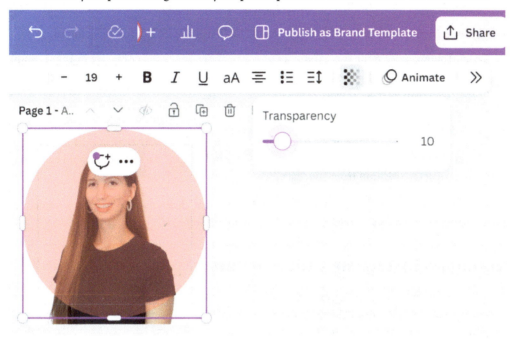

Figure 3.4: Changing the circle's transparency

8.   Eliminate the black circle, as we only needed it as a reference:

Figure 3.5: Finishing up your attention-grabbing profile picture

There's more...

If you are using a photo of yourself, here are a couple of tips on which photo to use or how to take it:

- Choose a high-quality photo. The photo should be sharp, ideally at a good resolution.

- Try and show your whole face. You may prefer to show only a part of it (for example, your eyes); however, it is psychologically proven that the human face attracts the observer's attention more. This is just advice though!

- Smile! This will convey positivity and confidence. Show your style and personality too.

- Choose a neutral background or, even better, a green screen, if you plan to change the background of your photo from time to time. However, keep in mind that the background should be simple and not distract attention from your face.

Once you have followed the steps previously detailed, I suggest you download the image at a resolution of no less than 500x500 px, as it could be grainy at a smaller resolution.

Creating an Instagram grid mockup

Creating a visually captivating Instagram grid requires planning and strategy. You want your profile to tell a story, showcase your brand identity, and ultimately, entice viewers to engage. This is where a mockup becomes your secret weapon.

A **mockup** is essentially a visual representation of your final design. Think of it as a blank canvas or a digital playground where you can experiment with various elements before committing them to your actual Instagram grid.

In this recipe, we'll dive into Canva to create a mockup for your social media feed. This lets you plan your content flow, experiment with layouts, and ensure everything looks cohesive before it goes live. No more scrambling to fix things last minute—a mockup can save you tons of time and help you or your client to get an idea of the final outcome!

Getting ready

To follow along with this recipe, you will need to open Pinterest (`pinterest.com`). We will look at the feed and find a color pattern that suits you. While browsing the feed, you may be asked to sign in to your account—if so, just sign in, or sign up if you don't have an account.

You will also need this Instagram feed mockup that I have prepared for you:

```
https://www.canva.com/design/DAF12zfN58c/1TnHXilpRtJRwf9mwPZLVw/
view?utm_content=DAF12zfN58c&utm_campaign=designshare&utm_
medium=link&utm_source=publishsharelink&mode=preview
```

How to do it...

To start customizing your Instagram profile, follow these steps:

1. Open Pinterest and search for `Instagram grid pattern` or `Instagram scheme feed`. From there, choose the grid color pattern that you like the most.

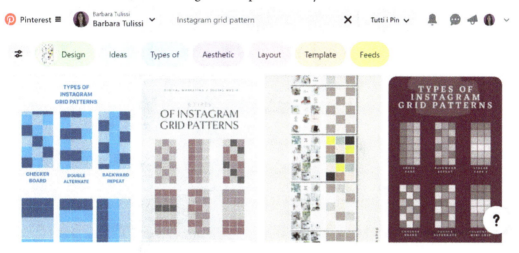

Figure 3.6: Instagram grid color schemes on Pinterest

If you do not find anything you like, you can pick one from the following infographic:

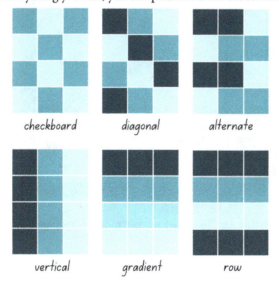

Figure 3.7: More Instagram grid color schemes

2. Then, to start replicating your chosen color pattern, open the Instagram mockup template that I provided in the *Getting ready* section. This is what it looks like:

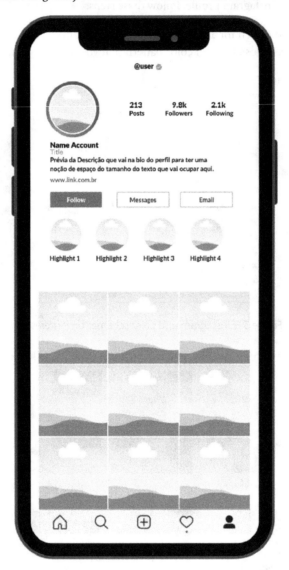

Figure 3.8: The Instagram feed mockup template

Once you open the link, click the **Use this template** button and it will create a copy of the project in Canva.

> **Note**
>
> I recommend that you save this template, so you have a backup copy for future use!

3. Now let's customize the template! Copy the color scheme pattern you found on Pinterest into your template, but use your brand's colors instead.

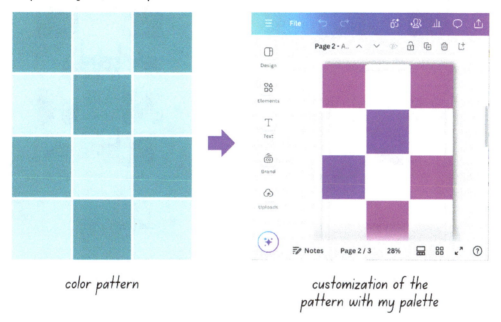

color pattern

customization of the
pattern with my palette

Figure 3.9: Incorporating the color scheme into the template

4. If you have already created content such as posts for your Instagram account in Canva, download them as `.png` or `.jpg` files. Then upload them from your desktop to Canva's **Uploads** section into your mockup project.

5.   Drag and drop each post onto a corresponding frame in the mockup, matching your content to the color scheme. In the following example, you can see that posts whose dominant color is violet have been placed on the purple tiles, and posts whose dominant color is white have been placed on the white tiles. If you don't have such a corresponding post, this is a great time to create one!

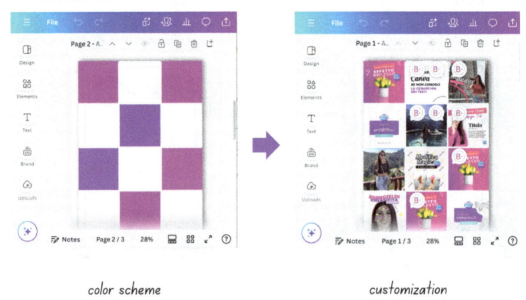

color scheme   customization

Figure 3.10: Moving your posts into the template

Note

If you have not created any posts, do not worry—you will learn how to do this in the next chapter.

6. In the template, customize the text with your profile name, bio, and so on to complete the mockup. Here is my result:

Figure 3.11: A completed Instagram grid mockup

7. Download your mockup as a `.png` or `.jpg` file to send it to your client or add it to a business presentation.

There's more...

As well as customizing your Instagram grid, you can also customize the images used for your Instagram story highlights. These highlights are a great way to organize and personalize your Instagram profile, and can be used to represent a specific theme, event, or project. You can see mine in the following screenshot:

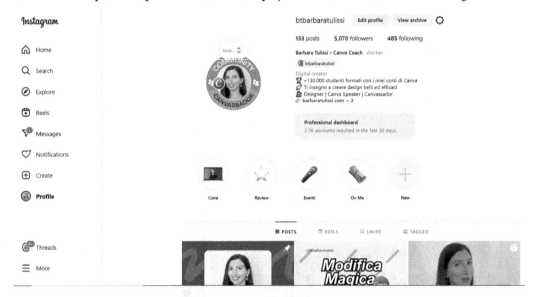

Figure 3.12: Create Instagram highlights

The main image used for each story highlight should clearly tell the viewer what the highlight is about, create a sense of continuity between your highlights, and help your followers better understand who you are and what you're about. Being a branding element, naturally, they must also use the colors, fonts, and style of your brand.

To create the images, you can use a similar method to the one used in the *Improving your profile picture* recipe earlier in the chapter:

1. Open a new project of size 1,080x1,920 px (the size of an Instagram story).

2. Press C on your keyboard to create a circle, then extend it across the entire page.

3. Color the circle black and lower the transparency to **10** to get an idea of the area that can be used for your Instagram highlight.

4. Now add your icon, emoji, or image, and color the background if needed.

Figure 3.13: Creating an Instagram highlight in Canva

5. Delete the circle.

6. Export the image as a `.png` or `.jpg` file, then go to Instagram and upload your new highlight.

Designing social covers for Facebook, LinkedIn, and YouTube

When we talk about social media covers, we are faced with a great opportunity: that of making a great impression right away. In fact, your profile image, combined with your social media cover, is like a business card that you can use to convey a message to a viewer of your profile.

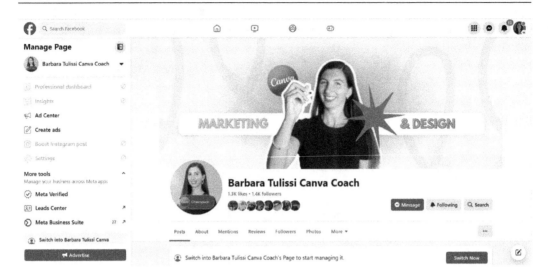

Figure 3.14: A Facebook cover

A social media cover that truly works is one that captures visitors' attention and encourages them to undertake an action, such as visiting your website, signing up for your newsletter, or purchasing your products or services.

However, covers are not so simple to create, as each social network has its own precise dimensions and cropping margins, which in turn can vary depending on the device used to view the cover. The following figure shows the measurements and their safety margins:

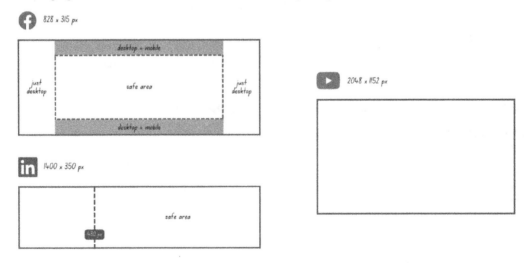

Figure 3.15: Social networks' banner dimensions

In this recipe, we will learn how to create covers for different social media platforms, considering their different dimensions and requirements.

How to do it...

In the following subsections, we will look at creating social covers for Facebook, LinkedIn, and YouTube. We will start with Facebook.

Facebook

When personalizing your Facebook profile, the first thing you are likely to do is upload a profile picture and a cover image. Firstly, if you run a business, I suggest uploading your logo; if you are a creator, I recommend uploading a portrait picture of yourself.

Then, to create your Facebook cover image, follow these steps:

1. Create a custom project with the dimensions 828x315 px, or search for a Facebook cover template that you like.

2. Go to **File | Settings**, and select **Show rulers**.

3. Use the vertical sliders to place one ruler around 127 px and another around 710 px. Then use the horizontal sliders to place one around 50 px and another around 260 px (you do not need to be extra precise with these ruler placements). This is the result:

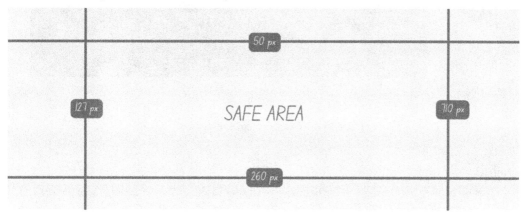

Figure 3.16: Safe area for your Facebook cover

Essentially, you've created a rectangular safe area within your design canvas. By placing text, images, and other crucial design elements within this area, you can be confident they'll be visible on both mobile and desktop devices.

4. Now add your content. Sometimes you may want to use a cover that conveys general information about your brand; however, since covers can be updated at any time, specific covers can be used in specific circumstances. For example, a pub may want to advertise a regular event, for example, an event they hold every Friday night.

    Therefore, you can upload an image of the pub or an image related to the event to Canva's **Uploads** section, then right-click on it and choose **Set Image as Background**.

    After that, you can add text boxes including the event name and details, and style the text with brand-/event-appropriate colors and fonts.

    Here is a possible result:

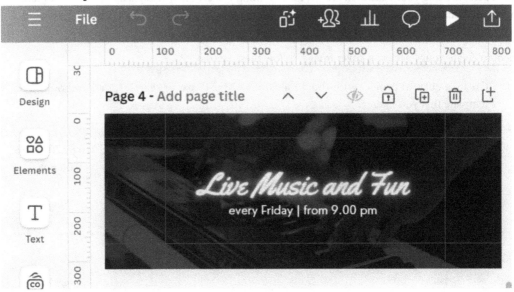

Figure 3.17: A Facebook cover in Canva

> **Note**
> There is no need to put the logo on the banner, as that should already be set as the profile picture.

5. Now you are ready to download your image as a .png file and upload it to Facebook!

6. Once you have uploaded the cover image to the social network, check it from a mobile and tablet to make sure that all the information is visible and that it is not too close to the margins. If there is a problem, you will need to go back to Canva and make sure all of the elements are inside the safe area.

LinkedIn

While it might be tricky to directly measure leads generated by your LinkedIn banner, creating a memorable banner can be the deciding factor between a profile visitor becoming a casual viewer or a valuable connection. After all, LinkedIn is about building networks and fostering professional relationships.

Think of it this way: you only have about three seconds to grab someone's attention on LinkedIn before they leave your profile. That's why this recipe is here, to help you craft a high-converting LinkedIn banner using Canva. By the end, you'll have a professional banner that pulls viewers in and inspires them to act on your profile.

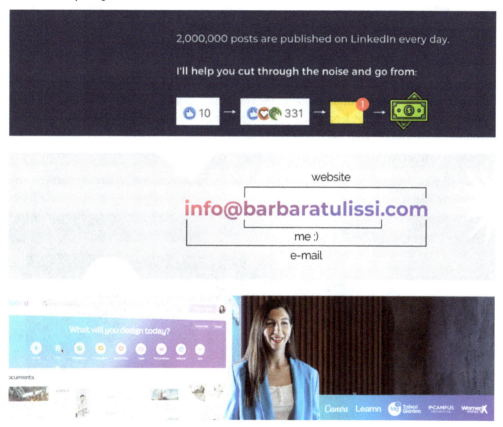

Figure 3.18: Examples of effective LinkedIn banners

To create a banner for LinkedIn, follow these steps:

1. Create a custom project with the dimensions 1,400x350 px, or search for a LinkedIn cover template that you like.

2. Go to **File | Settings**, and select **Show rulers**.

3. Now use the vertical sliders to place a ruler around 430 px—this will help you better understand what area is always visible (despite the device being used) and what is not.

Figure 3.19: LinkedIn banner safe area

4. Add a sentence or a call to action: it could be your vision or mission, your claim or quote. You can also add some useful information to the cover image, such as your email address or your Instagram profile handle. I suggest not adding your personal telephone number though, as you could get a lot of spam calls!

5. Customize it according to your mood board or your brand identity.

6. Place all your design elements on the right side of the banner since it is the only part that will always be visible.

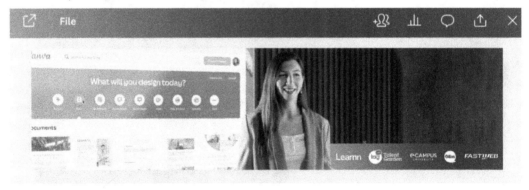

Figure 3.20: A LinkedIn banner in Canva

> **Note**
>
> Choose a background that is visually appealing but doesn't overpower your message. Solid colors, subtle gradients, or professional stock photos all work well. Remember, high-quality visuals are key! I like adding some elements for social proof (credibility) —such as the logos of brands you've worked for—to increase trust.

YouTube

Your YouTube banner is similar to a billboard for your channel, silently shouting to viewers what you're all about. But with so much competition, how do you make yours stand out? Don't worry, this recipe will guide you through creating a captivating banner that grabs viewers' attention and keeps them coming back for more.

Let's imagine we are the designers for a famous YouTuber, and that they asked us to re-design their banner to make potential subscribers better understand what they cover on their channels and how often they post new videos. To do this, we would take the following steps:

1. Create a custom project with the dimensions 2,048x1,152 px or use the search bar to find a YouTube cover template you like.

2. Go to **File | Settings**, and select **Show rulers**. Now use the vertical sliders to place a ruler around 333 px and another around 1,700 px. Then use the horizontal sliders to place a ruler around 360 px and another around 780 px. This will help you better understand what area is always visible (despite the device being used), and what is not.

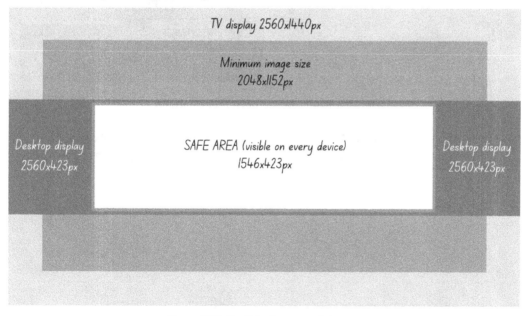

Figure 3.21: YouTube banner safety area

3. Choose a high-quality image or illustration that reflects the channel's theme. In this case, I chose a solid color and added some geometric elements to it to create a custom background.

4. Then add a concise headline. This is the viewer's first impression, so make it count! Similar to the approach for LinkedIn and Facebook covers, use a short, catchy headline that tells viewers exactly what kind of content the YouTuber creates. Think of it as a mini elevator pitch for their channel.

    In this case, I like to make the channel's topic very clear and include information about how often the creator uploads/goes live. Also, adding information about the YouTuber's other social media platforms will encourage viewers to follow them on other platforms too.

5. I also recommend including an image of yourself in your cover image, particularly if your profile picture is your channel's logo. This makes the cover feel more personal and gives the viewer an idea of who you are.

6. Make sure all of the text and elements fit in the safe areas.

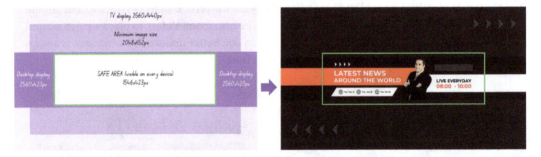

Figure 3.22: From the safe area to customizing the YouTube banner

7. As always, double-check the cover once you have uploaded it to the channel cover. Check it on different devices to make sure the text is readable, and all of the design elements are visible (i.e., are within the safe area).

4

Crafting Engaging
Social Content

Want your social media presence to pack a punch? This chapter equips you with the know-how to craft engaging content in Canva, the design platform that empowers anyone to become a social media wiz. We'll delve into practical techniques for creating eye-catching graphics and posts that stop the scroll and spark conversations.

Think of this chapter as your recipe book for social media success. I'll provide you with some useful recipes for crafting specific brand assets, such as social posts, carousels, and stories, all within the user-friendly Canva interface. Through these recipes, you will be able to confidently produce content that resonates with your audience and elevates your social media game.

In this chapter, we will cover the following recipes:

- Taking a single social media post to the next level
- Creating a carousel post
- Creating an animated swipe-bounce effect for your carousel
- Creating a collage post layout
- Creating a mosaic effect for Instagram
- Creating a social media story
- Creating a meme

Taking a single social media post to the next level

Craving a visually stunning single post for your social media feed? Look no further! In this recipe, we will take an initial design, and you'll whip up a mouthwatering social media post that will have your followers reaching for their phones and hitting that like button. So, grab your design tools (metaphorically speaking!), and let's get cooking (with pixels)!

Getting ready

Before we start thinking about creating our post, there is one important piece of advice I want to give: *always respect lateral margins.*

Margins visually separate the content from the edge of the canvas, preventing a cluttered feel and guiding the viewer's eye toward the central focus of your post. They also improve readability, ensuring your text is comfortably within the boundaries of the post and that no text is cut off.

Here's how to set them up:

1. Open a project (the size doesn't matter).

2. Go to the top menu and select **File**.

3. From the options, select **View settings**, and then **Show margins**.

    A dashed line all around your page will appear, which are your margins:

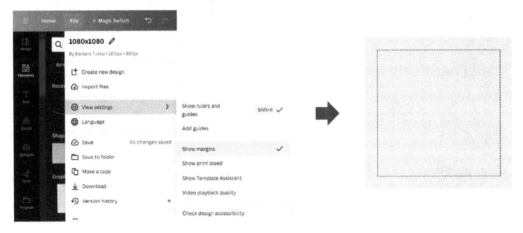

Figure 4.1: How to show margins

How to do it...

To get started, we need that initial post. For that, let's introduce you to my personal favorite method – "stealing like an artist"!

"Stealing like an artist" in graphic design means learning from existing work, not copying it. It's about finding inspiration, analyzing successful designs, and using these insights to create something original. It's about building on the work of others to develop your unique style.

To do this, go to the **Templates** section of Canva. Pick a few templates that catch your eye, focusing on elements that resonate with you. This could be anything from a captivating font style to a well-placed image or a color scheme that pops. Then, drag and drop the desired elements from the template page directly onto your project. Alternatively, you can copy and paste them for a seamless transfer.

By using pre-designed templates as a source of inspiration, you're essentially "stealing" the good stuff – fonts, colors, layouts – and incorporating them into your own unique creation. This method ignites your creative spark and helps you overcome that initial blank-page hurdle.

Let's see what I have done. I have taken the example of a travel agency (which I will use for the rest of the recipe):

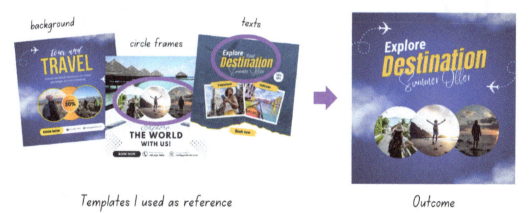

Figure 4.2: The "stealing like an artist" method applied in Canva

> **Remember**
>
> The next time you find yourself creatively blocked, remember that there's no shame in "stealing" a bit of inspiration. With a dash of resourcefulness and the power of Canva's tools, you can transform borrowed elements into something entirely your own.

Okay, so now you've used the "stealing like an artist" method and assembled your initial post. Now comes the magic touch: customization!

Remember, whether you're a free-version Canva user or a Pro subscriber, we'll cover the customization process for both scenarios, ensuring your post shines bright!

If you are using Canva Free

Let's look at what the customization process looks like for those of you using a free version of Canva:

1. With your project window open, go back to the main dashboard. This way, you will have the two tabs open side by side on your browser.

Figure 4.3: Mood board tab and single post tab

2. From the dashboard, open your brand identity, color palette, or mood board (if you do not know what I am talking about, go back to *Chapter 2* for a refresher).

3. Now, customize your colors. Let's say you've chosen a stunning turquoise shade on your travel agency mood board. Here's how to incorporate it into your post:

    I.   Locate the color box on your mood board that holds the perfect turquoise hue.

    II.   With a click, you'll reveal the exact color code for that turquoise shade. It might look something like #13EECC.

    III. Within your post, select the element you want to adjust. This could be a background box, text color, or even an element you "stole" from a template. Simply copy the color code from your mood board, and then in your new project, select the element you want to color.

    IV.   Click on the color box, then the rainbow circle, and paste the color code.

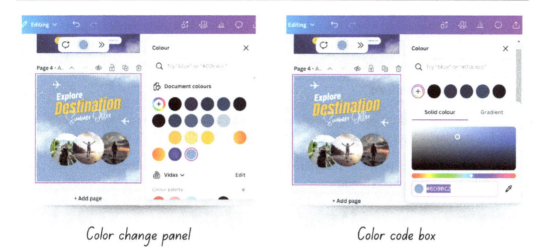

Color change panel   Color code box

Figure 4.4: Using the color box

4. In your mood board, you can also discover what font your "stolen" reference post is using. Simply click on the text box containing the font and Canva will display the font name. Note it down and then apply it to your own project.

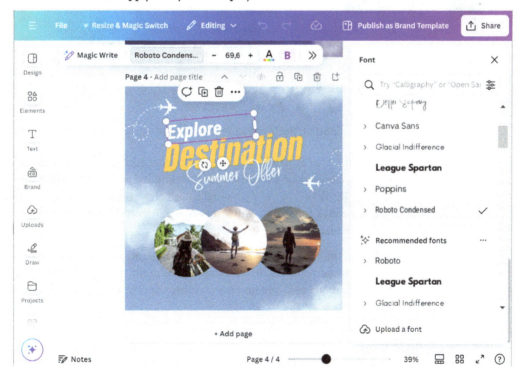

Figure 4.5: Finding your reference's font name

While Canva's free version offers a solid foundation, you might find it slow after a while. To supercharge your creativity and boost productivity, consider upgrading to Canva Pro. It's an investment that can save you precious time and elevate your designs to the next level.

If you are using Canva Pro

Let's consider the case in which you purchased the Canva membership. If you have already added all the style information to your Canva brand kit, then customizing will be a piece of cake:

1. With your post open, go to the **Template** section and select the **Style** tab. From here, you can find the brand kit option (**Brand**).

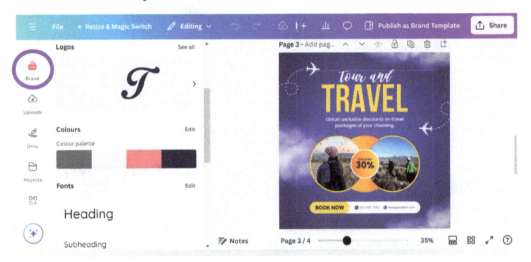

Figure 4.6: Spotting the brand kit option in Canva

The brand kit eliminates the need to constantly copy and paste color codes from a mood board, saving you time and ensuring consistency. This allows you to define and store all the colors you use for your brand identity. Think of it as your personal color palette library. When you are about to customize your template's colors, you will just need to click on the color box to find your palette's colors readily available at your fingertips.

2. In the **Brand** section, click on the color palette and Canva will randomly replace all the colors of your template with the ones of your palette. You can click as many times as you need to explore different color combinations until you find your favorite one. Then, you can apply that color palette to your post.

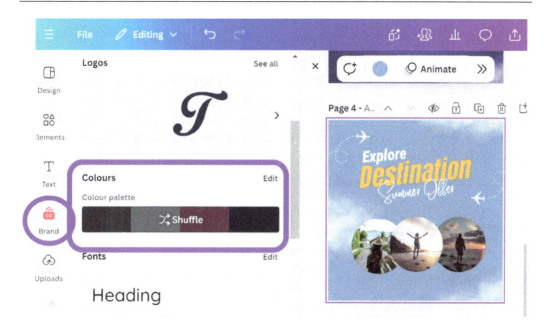

Figure 4.7: Customizing your colors using the brand kit

3. You can do the same for fonts. Once you set them into your brand kit, just click on your text box and you will find your brand's fonts in the **Font** panel.

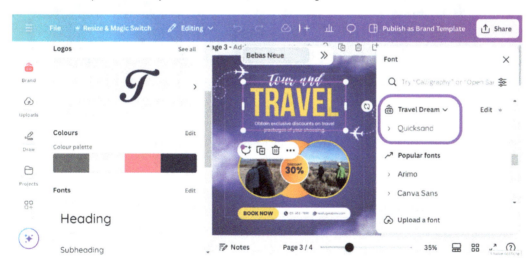

Figure 4.8: Customizing your text using the brand kit

Creating a carousel post

Carousels are a powerful tool for grabbing attention and engaging your audience. Unlike static posts, they offer a horizontal, swipeable format that allows you to showcase multiple pieces of information, tell a story, or guide users through a process in a series of slides. Think of them as a mini-website within a social media post. With each swipe, viewers unveil a new panel, keeping them interested and engaged.

Instagram is probably the most obvious place you can use to post a carousel, but you can also post them on Facebook and LinkedIn.

A well-structured carousel is key to maximizing engagement. Here's a breakdown of the ideal format:

- **Cover slide**: This is your first impression. It should grab attention with a captivating visual and a clear title.

- **Hook slide**: Briefly explain the cover and entice viewers to swipe for more.

- **Content slides**: This is where you expand on your message. You can have up to 10 slides on Instagram and an unlimited number on LinkedIn.

- **Call to action (CTA)**: Wrap up your carousel with a clear and specific call to action, prompting viewers to take the next step, whether it's visiting your website, making a purchase, or following you for more content.

COVER   HOOK   CONTENT SLIDES   CTA

Figure 4.9: Carousel structure

Now that we understand the power of carousels, let's explore how to create them in Canva.

> **Note**
> You can take a closer look at the carousel through this link: `https://www.instagram.com/p/C3UhzoLIhKG/?img_index=1`

How to do it...

There are two main methods you can choose from, depending on your desired outcome:

- **Slide carousel**: This is a classic carousel format with distinct slides separated by borders
- **Seamless carousel**: This method creates a more unified look where the slides flow together

We'll delve into the specifics of both methods, helping you choose the perfect approach for your next social media masterpiece.

Method 1 – slide carousel

Let's create a slide carousel. Start a new project, either using a template or a blank page. If you are using a blank page, you can decide whether to open a file measuring 1,080x1,080 px or one measuring 1,080x1,350 px. As we said when creating a post, creating a post measuring 1,080x1,350 px will mean users will likely spend more time on your content, as the vertical structure allows you to scroll the content more than once.

However, what I haven't revealed to you yet is that the vertical structure doesn't allow you to have a clear preview of how your content will look once published in the feed. As you can see from the following figure, the bottom and top edges are cut off so inserting particularly important information along the margins would not make sense as they would not be seen.

Figure 4.10: Instagram post dimensions

That is why I recommend following these instructions to create a slide carousel and make sure you do not place information among the margins:

1.   With your project open, press *R* on your keyboard to create a rectangle.

2.   Click on the diagonal transformation point of the square and pull the upper right corner up to the project's edge. Then, repeat the operation with the lower left corner (note that the square must have the same length side; make sure you have not created a rectangle!).

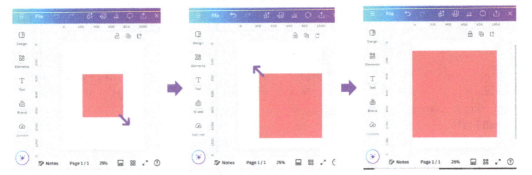

Figure 4.11: Expanding the rectangle for your carousel

3.   Next, make sure that the rectangle is perfectly centered in the middle of the page – you can check this by moving it with the mouse until the horizontal and the vertical purple lines appear.

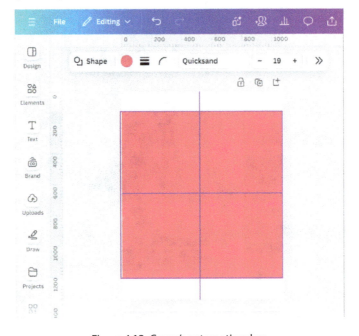

Figure 4.12: Canva's automatic rulers

4. In your project, click **File** and select **Show rulers and guides**.

5. Some rulers will appear, one vertical and one horizontal. Pull the horizontal one down until it matches the lower side of the square, and then release it. Next, pull the horizontal ruler down again so the second line matches the upper side of the square. You don't need to touch the horizontal ruler.

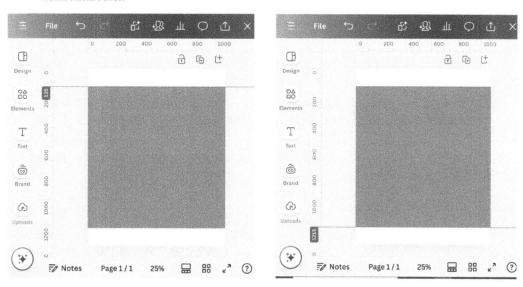

Figure 4.13: Setting rulers for your carousel

6. Now, eliminate the square we created. What you will be left with are two horizontal purple lines that mark the area within which you can place all the main information (i.e., the one that will then be shown in the preview of your Instagram feed).

You can see what we have done so far, as illustrated here:

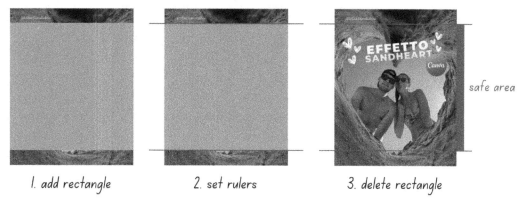

1. add rectangle   2. set rulers   3. delete rectangle

Figure 4.14: Creating a safe area for your design

> **Note**
>
> Carousels on LinkedIn can have various sizes, such as a presentation (1,920x1,080 px), and you do not need to apply the square trick for the first slide.

7. Now, you can start adding text, shapes, images, or a video to create your first slide.

8. Once you have created your first slide, click **Add page** to create a new page (the carousel's second slide).

9. Hide the rulers by going to **File** and unchecking the **Show rulers and guides** option. You don't need the rulers anymore – they are just necessary to better display slide one in the Instagram feed.

10. Next, click on **File** and select **Show margins** (even if you do not need any ruler from now on, this does not mean you do not need to respect margins).

11. Feel free to create your own design and unleash your creativity for your carousel! Once you are done with the second slide, you can keep going, adding pages/slides and customizing them to finish your carousel.

Method 2 – seamless carousel

Compared to the previous method where each slide of the carousel is different, this method is recommended if you want to insert elements of continuity within your carousel, such as the same background in all the slides. To do this, follow these steps:

1. First, prepare the contents of your slides in advance. How many slides will you make? Well, suppose I want to make 8 in total, I will have to multiply this number by 1000 px, which is the length of a single slide. 8 x 1000 = 8,000px so my project will be 8,000x1,080 px.

> **Note**
>
> Remember that Canva has limits. At the time of writing, it is not possible to create projects larger than 8000 px.

2. Once you open the project, go to **File** and select **Show rulers and guides** – even with this method, you will still need to know where one slide ends and another begins, so you will have to reset the rulers.

3. Using the vertical ruler, drop a line at each slide break. We're splitting the 8,000 px wide carousel into 8, so release the first line at 1,000 px, the second at 2,000 px, the third at 3,000 px, and so on.

Figure 4.15: Splitting the carousel

If you are struggling to place the rulers at the perfect point, you can use the zoom option in the bottom-right corner, which allows you to enlarge the pixels and pick the right number.

4. Once the carousel image has been split, download the carousel as a PNG file.

5. Then, let's head to `pinetools.com`. **PineTools** is a handy resource for anyone who needs to complete quick tasks related to math, text, colors, images, dates, randomness, or files. Here, we want to search for an option called **Split Image**.

6. Once the **Split Image** option has been found, upload your carousel, select the number of slides you want to split, and download the individual slides.

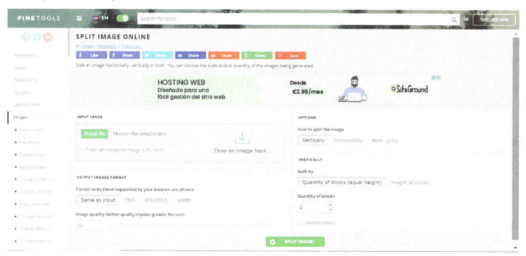

Figure 4.16: PineTools

Creating a seamless carousel often involves a back-and-forth process between Canva and other platforms. While this might seem counterintuitive, it's a creative workaround that allows for maximum design control.

There's more...

Regardless of which method you choose, you should be able to upload your carousels to Instagram with ease. Once you downloaded the carousel slides from PineTools, they will be available as `.png` or `.jpg` to upload to Instagram.

However, if you want to upload your carousels to LinkedIn, you need to make sure you download them as PDFs. Also, if you want to plan to use a continuous carousel on LinkedIn, you will need to do the following:

1. Return to Canva and open a project with dimensions of 1,080x1,080 px.
2. Load all the individual images downloaded from PineTools and put them in chronological order.
3. Export the project as a standard PDF.

Creating an animated swipe-bounce effect for your carousel

The **swipe effect** is a type of animation that can be inserted directly onto the cover / first slide of a carousel to indicate to the viewer that the post is a carousel and can therefore be scrolled. The effect contains a little bounce, tempting you to scroll through the post.

Take a look at this example to get an idea of what I mean – `https://www.instagram.com/p/C1-02eSvgU4/` – and then follow along with this recipe to create this effect.

Getting ready

Make sure you have created a carousel. However, keep in mind that the swipe effect only works with a *slide* carousel (not a seamless one).

How to do it...

To create our animated swipe effect for your carousel, do the following:

1. With your slide carousel open, go to the top menu, click **Download**, and download the second page of the carousel as a `.jpg` or `.png` file.
2. Once downloaded, import it into the **Uploads** section of Canva.

3. Go back to the first page and insert the image, placing it along the right edge of the cover.

4. Click on the imported image, go to **Animate**, and choose **Create an animation**.

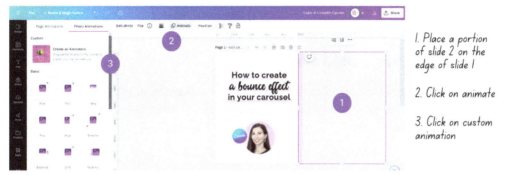

1. Place a portion of slide 2 on the edge of slide 1

2. Click on animate

3. Click on custom animation

Figure 4.17: Navigating to the Create an Animation option

Now, you can do the following:

*   **Touch and drag (if you are using a tablet or phone)**: With your finger, press and hold the image, then drag it along the desired path to create the swipe animation.

*   **Shift and drag**: Click and hold the image while pressing the *Shift* key. Drag the image along the desired path to create the swipe animation.

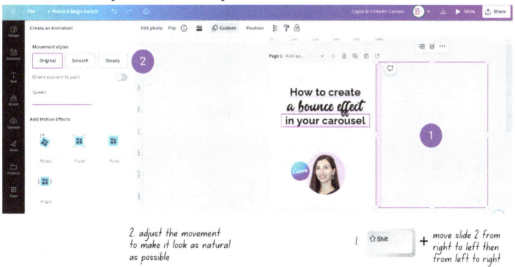

2. adjust the movement to make it look as natural as possible

1. Shift + move slide 2 from right to left then from left to right

Figure 4.18: Animating the carousel

5. Finally, to ensure that the animation can be seen, export the *cover* as a `.mp4` file and upload that file to Instagram. Note that Instagram will play the video in a loop, so you don't need to set the animation duration in Canva. All the other slides can be uploaded in the `.png` or `.jpg` format.

Creating a collage post layout

Creating a collage post layout can significantly enhance the visual appeal of your posts, creating a more engaging experience for viewers. It can also replicate some of the benefits of the carousel format, which is only available on Facebook if you sponsor your content through Meta ads.

When it comes to collage posts, here are some example formats:

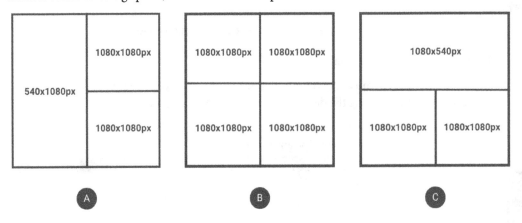

Figure 4.19: Facebook special formats

These formats are very simple to create in Canva and if you follow this recipe, you will be able to craft them properly. Let's create one together!

How to do it...

Suppose we want to create format *A* shown in *Figure 3.19*:

1. Open a Canva project with a size of 540x1,080 px and start designing your content.

2. Open another project with a size of 1,080x1,080 px nearby (the same as a square Instagram post) and design your content there too.

3. Repeat *Step 2* two more times, designing two more 1,080x1,080 px squares.

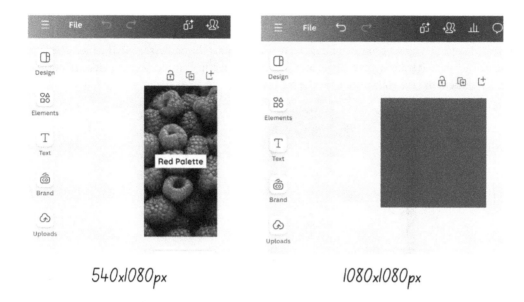

540x1080px   1080x1080px

Figure 4.20: Creating the A format squares

4. Download both the vertical and the square slides as PNG files.

5. Open Facebook, create a post, and add all the images here. In the post preview, Facebook should give you a realistic preview of how the post will appear.

Figure 4.21: A collage post, posted on Facebook

Creating a mosaic effect for Instagram

Ever wished your Instagram profile could grab attention amidst the endless feed? The mosaic effect is your secret weapon! It transforms a single image into a captivating puzzle, piquing viewers' curiosity and enticing them to visit your profile for the big reveal.

Normal content

3x3 mosaic at the beginning of my new profile

Figure 4.22: Mosaic effect at the beginning of my Instagram profile

This recipe will show you how to create stunning mosaic posts in Canva, perfect for launching a new account or announcing a brand refresh. It's a strategic way to stand out, spark conversation, and leave a lasting impression. Let's get started!

How to do it...

Let's imagine we are starting a new Instagram profile and populating our feed with nine posts. These nine posts, when looked at all together, will create one mosaic post that introduces who we are to our future audience:

1. Open a project in Canva with the measurements 3,240x3,240 px. This will be the reference size for your 3x3 mosaic piece.

2. Design the image you want to transform into a mosaic. It can be a photo, illustration, or even a text graphic. Keep it clear and visually appealing, as it will be split into smaller squares.

> **Note**
>
> Take also into account that mosaics work best with simpler images or bold colors. Complex photos with intricate details might lose their impact when broken down into smaller squares.

3. Once created, download the file as a `.png` file.

4. Visit `https://pinetools.com/` and find the **Split Image** option.

5. Upload the image you designed in Canva. In the **Rows** and **Columns** section, enter 3 for both options – this will ensure your image is split into a perfect 3x3 grid.

6. Click **Split Image** and it will generate nine individual squares from your original image.

7. Then, click **Download** to save each image square. PineTools will usually number them for easy reference.

8. Now, hop on to Instagram! To make sure that the mosaic is uploaded correctly, you will need to upload the images backward; so, you will need to upload the bottom-right image first and work your way up to the top-left image. Check out the following illustration to guide you:

Figure 4.23: The order to post your mosaic images on Instagram

> **Note**
>
> Crafting a visually striking Instagram feed requires careful planning. While a mosaic effect can be captivating, it demands significant time and effort. Maintaining consistency across multiple posts can be restrictive, and even minor errors can disrupt the overall aesthetic. Additionally, the algorithm may favor more diverse feeds. Ultimately, I suggest you weigh this decision against these factors and your overall content strategy.

Creating a social media story

Stories differ from posts in that they have a limited duration of time (usually 24 hours) and have a vertical format of 1,080x1,920 px.

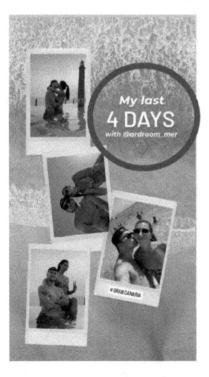

The circled part was made directly on Instagram

Figure 4.24: Create a story in Canva for Instagram (or Facebook)

Before continuing, there are two things to note about stories:

- Keep in mind that on Instagram, Facebook, TikTok, and other social networks, you can insert stickers and texts into your stories, such as the one circled in *Figure 4.24* (that was created on Instagram, not Canva)

- Some social networks could cut the margins of your story or fill them with superimposed icons, which is why I advise you to always maintain a large safety margin and concentrate the focus of your message in the center of the screen

Figure 4.25: Story margins on Instagram

In this recipe, we will assume you want to create a story containing multiple photos from your recent holiday, like my example back in *Figure 4.24*.

Getting ready

To help you out with the recipe, I have created a collage template to help you: https://www.canva.com/design/DAGDaamJaaA/iBOFDC7JWKSUYG4NcN34uQ/view?utm_content=DAGDaamJaaA&utm_campaign=designshare&utm_medium=link&utm_source=publishsharelink&mode=preview.

How to do it...

To create a story, follow these instructions:

1. Open a Canva project measuring 1,080x1,920 px.

2. Go to **File | Settings** and check **Show margins** to design everything inside the margins.

3. In the **Options** menu, choose **Templates** and search for `collage`. From here, you can choose your favorite collage template. Alternatively, you can use the template I provided in the *Getting ready* section.

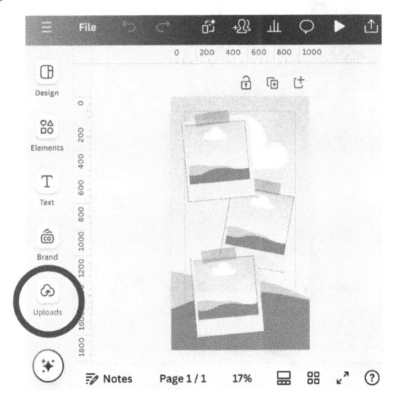

Figure 4.26: Our collage template in action

4. Then, to insert images into frames of the collage, all you need to do is upload your photos in the **Uploads** section and drag the photos inside the frames.

5. Now, download your story collage as a `.png` file.

6. Open Instagram (or Facebook) and start uploading your story. Before publishing, you can use the story editor to add text, stickers, and so on. Once happy, press **Upload**!

Creating a meme

Memes often take the form of images, videos, or text shared widely online. They are typically humorous and often satirize current events or cultural phenomena. They are a way to express yourself and a great way to make our audience empathize and interact with our brands.

Figure 4.27: Canva meme (for the record, Canva is extremely easy to use!)

That's why Canva is full of templates for creating beautiful memes. Despite that, we are not going to use any template. Let's create one from scratch instead.

How to do it...

To create a meme in Canva, follow these steps:

1. Open a project of the size most convenient for the platform you will be posting on. For example, if the meme will be posted on Facebook or Instagram, use the 1,080x1,080 px format.

2. Press *R* on your keyboard to create a rectangle. Set its color to black and size it so that it is longer than it is tall.

3. Place the rectangle at the top of the page, duplicate it, and place it at the bottom of the page.

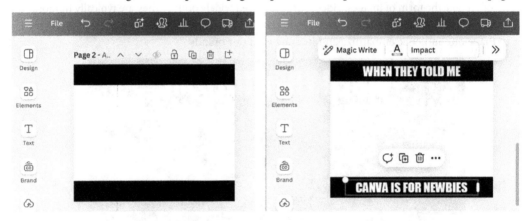

Figure 4.28: Adding the rectangles

> **Note**
>
> What we could do is set the whole background of the project to black, and then place an image in the middle. However, by creating the two rectangles, we give ourselves more control over the design – if we want to further customize the black rectangle shaping the borders or color them separately (for example, one in orange and one in black), we can do that.

4. Create a text box by pressing *T* on the keyboard and write the text of my meme.

5. Set the text's font to **Anton**, change the color to white, and set its size to one that allows you to fit the text nicely in the rectangle.

6. Move the text box on top of the rectangle.

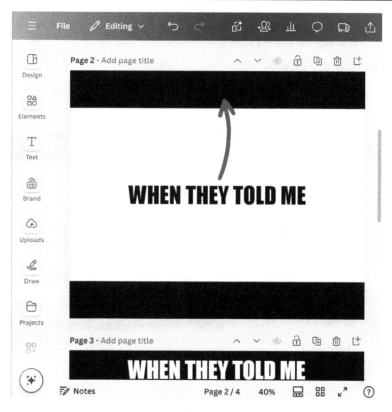

Figure 4.29: Adding the meme text

7.   Duplicate the text box, add some more text, and move it over the bottom rectangle.

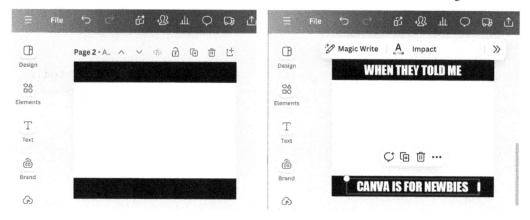

Figure 4.30: Adding more meme text

8. Now, go to the **Elements** menu, and under the **Frames** section, select the rectangular frame that will extend across the entire page.

9. Decrease its size to make it match the two black rectangles.

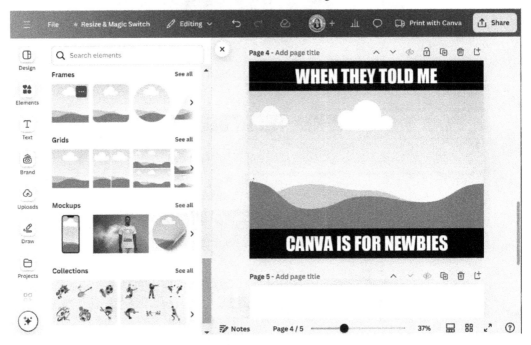

Figure 4.31: Adding a frame to our meme

10. Insert an image into the frame, and there you have it – a completed meme.

There's more...

In addition to Canva, there are many meme generators that you can use online, for example, `https://www.iloveimg.com/meme-generator`. However, my advice is always to create personalized memes, using photos of yourself or your team, and never images covered by copyright!

5

Creating
Impactful Presentations

Alright, let's get your presentations sizzling! This chapter is your one-stop shop for transforming those snoozy slideshows into show-stopping presentations.

Here, we'll crack the code on design principles, mastering everything from visual storytelling to data visualization. We'll learn how to transform your presentations into compelling stories that engage and inspire, as well as use charts, graphs, and infographics to present complex data in a clear and visually appealing manner.

Forget templates and cookie-cutter slides – we're building presentations that resonate, leaving your audience hungry for more. So, buckle up and get ready to unleash your inner rockstar presenter!

Here are the recipes that we will cover in this chapter:

- Creating a presentation for a client
- Creating a presentation from a document
- Visualizing data better in your presentations
- Using infographics in your presentations
- Utilizing animations in your presentations
- Presenting presentations in Canva
- Importing, exporting, and sharing presentations

Creating a presentation for a client

Client presentations – they can be the make-or-break moment in landing that desired project. But fear not; this recipe will help you whip up a killer presentation using Canva. Here, we'll dissect the key ingredients of a presentation, from crafting a clear narrative to using design elements that pack a punch.

Getting ready

Before we dive into the design tools and dazzling visuals, let's take a step back and understand the most important ingredient in this recipe: your client. This presentation is about them, and their needs.

Here's the secret sauce: *empathy*. What are your client's goals? What kind of visual style resonates with their brand? Think about their website, social media presence, or any marketing materials they have. Matching their existing visual language builds trust and shows you've taken the time to understand their world.

Having said that, a subtle nod to your brand identity with your logo placed strategically on the first slide sets the stage, while including your contact details at the end enforces who you are and who to speak to if they want more information. Consider it your professional signature on this delectable presentation.

To get ready, I suggest you start with a template. Browse the templates to find one you like. In this recipe, I will be imagining that the presentation is for a vet shop, so I will search for `dog presentation`:

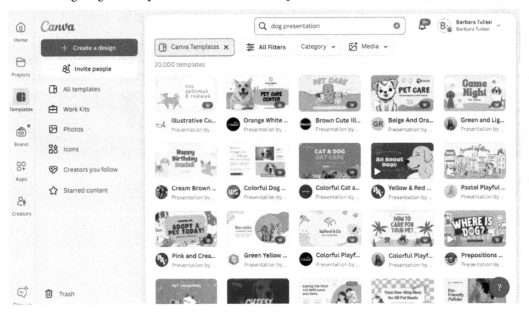

Figure 5.1: Finding a template

How to do it...

As mentioned, I will imagine that I am creating a presentation for a vet shop that has hired us for its new social media strategy. Our presentation will have five slides:

- *Slide 1*: This will be the cover of your presentation, which aims to grab the client's attention.

- *Slide 2*: This is the introduction to your topic, which is usually a breakdown of the presentation's main ideas.

- *Slide 3*: As we are pretending to create a social media strategy, on this slide we want to state the target audience for the strategy: who is the strategy aimed at? What do they desire? What do they fear?

- *Slide 4*: Here, we want to dive deeper into the core of your presentation, explaining the juicy details about your social media strategy.

- *Slide 5*: Finally, don't forget a strong call to action! You can invite you audience to connect with you on LinkedIn or to keep talking via email or in person.

With your template ready, let's start creating the slides:

1. *Slide 1: The Cover*:

    I.   Use the **Photos** tab to find a high-quality image of a happy pet or the vet clinic.

    II.   Add a text box (shortcut *T*) and write a clear and concise title (something like Social Media Strategy).

    III.   Enhance the visual hierarchy with appropriate font sizes and styles.

    IV.   Incorporate the client's logo using the **Uploads** section.

    V.   Apply brand colors (using the eyedropper tool or Brand Kit, if available).

Figure 5.2: Designing the cover slide

2. *Slide 2: Introduction and Overview*:

    I.   Add a text box (*T*) and write a slide title – it can be as simple as Intro.

    II.   Browse the **Photo** tab again for another lovely dog picture.

III.   Add another text box and write some content to introduce the topic. You could even use Canva's Magic Write option. In the toolbar, click **Magic Write**, then **Custom prompt** from the dropdown.

Figure 5.3: Finding the Custom prompt option

IV.   In the text box that appears, type `Introduce the vet shop and outline the presentation`, and click **Generate**:

Figure 5.4: Generating text with Magic Write

> **Note**
>
> Since Magic Write is a Pro feature of Canva, you can also use a free tool, which is Gemini, from Google. Just type `Gemini` in Google's search bar and, in the prompt bar, add your prompt. Once the output has been generated, you can copy it and paste it within your Canva presentation.

3. *Slide 3: Defining the Target Audience*:

    I.   Add text boxes for the slide title and body text.

    II.   Add some images too, or even a GIF. Yes, you can add a GIF to your slide with a handy Canva integration with Giphy. Simply click on **Apps** and type `Giphy` in the search bar. Once you have opened Giphy, use some strategic keywords to search for a hilarious GIF (e.g., `dog` or `funny dog`). Once you have found one, just click on it to add it to your slide.

Figure 5.5: Using Giphy

> **Note**
>
> The effectiveness of GIFs as a marketing tool depends on your brand's image and target audience. While GIFs can be fun and engaging, consider whether they align with your overall messaging. If you're unsure, revisit *Chapter 2* to understand your brand's tone of voice and determine if GIFs are a suitable fit.

4.   *Slide 4: The Social Media Strategy*:

To illustrate information such as a social media strategy, use a table or grid layout to organize platform-specific goals and tactics:

I.   Select the **Elements** tab on the left-hand toolbar.

II.   Find the **Table** tool (it's the grid icon). Click on it to reveal various table layout options.

III. Select the number of rows and columns needed for your table. Canva offers a range of pre-set options to suit different datasets.

IV.   Select the first row and change its fill color. This helps differentiate the column titles from the main text.

V.   Enter your data into the table cells.

Figure 5.6: Adding a table

5.   *Slide 5: Call to Action*:

This is where you want to include your contact information. For this, use Brandfetch, which helps you find brand logos. Within it, you can find, for example, the official logos of TikTok, Instagram, and many others:

I.   Open **Apps**, type `Brandfetch` in the search bar, and select it.

II.   With the **Brandfetch** tab, type the name of the social media logo you need (e.g., Facebook) into the search bar.

III.   Choose the logo you like the most and add it to your design by dragging it into your design.

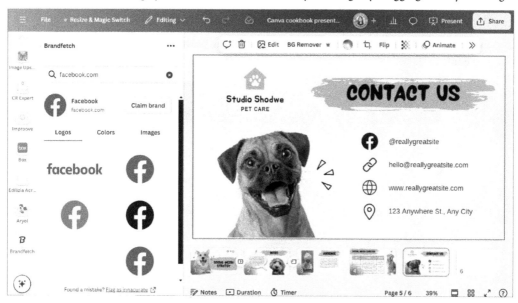

Figure 5.7: Using Brandfetch

There's more...

Ever felt overwhelmed staring at a blank Canva slide, or unsure which template to use? We've all been there. But fret no more, because there's another feature – the **Layouts** feature. Think of it as a magic toolbox overflowing with pre-designed slide layouts, each one brimming with creative potential.

These layouts aren't just pretty pictures. They're strategically crafted to showcase different types of content, such as text, images, and charts. Need a slide to introduce your team? There's a layout for that. Want to present data with punch? Layouts have you covered.

But wait, there's more! The Layouts feature is like a design chameleon, adapting to your existing style. Canva cleverly analyzes the colors and fonts you've already used in your presentation and previews the layouts with those selections. This means seamless integration – no more jarring clashes between your chosen layout and your overall design scheme. It's a time-saving, creativity-boosting win-win!

Here's how to add layouts to your presentation:

1. With your presentation open in Canva, add a new page.

2. In the **Design** panel in the left-hand menu, click on the **Layouts** tab. A lot of new blank slides will come up.

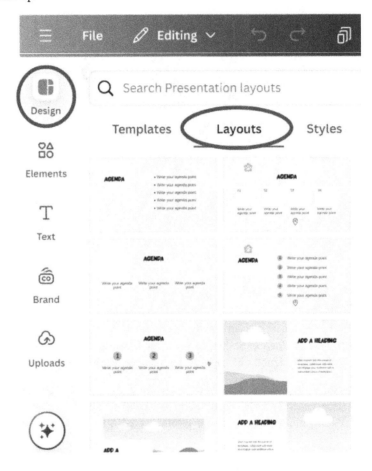

Figure 5.8: The Layout tab

As you might see from the **Layout** panel, Canva already shows the slide preview with the colors and fonts it detects from your actual presentation so you can get an idea of the outcome.

3. Find a layout that complements your additional message and click on it. Suppose you must add a slide about data. Scroll through the **Layout** panel to find your favorite one. Once you have chosen one, click on your layout to add it to a new page of your presentation.

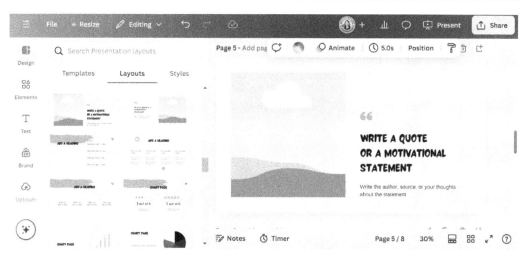

Figure 5.9: Adding a layout

4. Now, customize the content. Replace the placeholder text and images with your client's information!

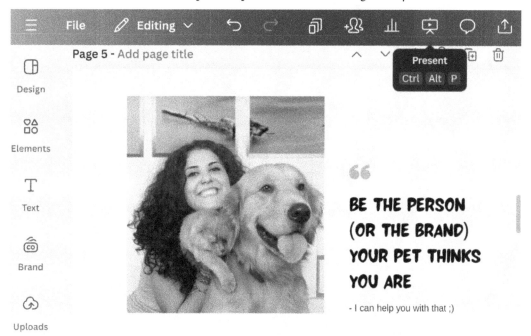

Figure 5.10: Customizing the layout

5.   As an extra tip, on the **Design** panel, next to the **Layouts** tab, is the **Styles** tab. Here, you will find your Brand Kit (if you have Canva Pro) and other suggested palettes and font combos that you can freely use by just clicking on them.

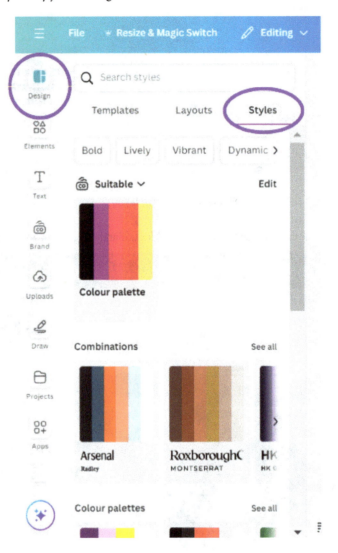

Figure 5.11: The Styles tab

Now, imagine you need to change a color that you have used throughout all the slides. With a defined visual identity, you can edit that color in one click, and Canva automatically updates it across all your slides – a true time-saver! The same goes for fonts. With one change, your entire presentation reflects the update.

There's even more...

Now, it's time to review your presentation! Since creating presentations for a client can be a little difficult and overwhelming, I have created a checklist for you. Check it out every time you complete your presentation!

Element to review	Done?
Have you used the client's colors/font /imagery?	
Have you checked for typos?	
Have you read it out loud from the beginning to the end? Does it make sense? Is the text fluent?	
Is the text formatted? For example, have you highlighted keywords in bold or used italics for quotes?	
Have you considered the amount of information per slide? Have you provided too much information? (A maximum of three concepts per slide is a good rule.)	
Is the text legible (for example, no blue text on a dark background)? Is the text big enough for people to read comfortably (particularly for people who may have sight impairments, for example)?	
Does your presentation still work/look good on different devices (e.g., a phone)?	

Creating a presentation from a document

Imagine you are on an airplane and you come up with a fantastic presentation idea. Unfortunately, Canva needs an internet connection to use, and airplane Wi-Fi can be expensive/unreliable. Instead, you start writing your notes in Word. When you arrive home, you now want to convert your notes into a Canva presentation. But how?

Enter the secret weapon of this recipe: Canva's **Magic Switch** feature. This recipe reveals how to seamlessly convert that Word document (or any text document) into a stunning presentation – all within the familiar and user-friendly confines of Canva.

How to do it...

Follow these steps to use the Magic Switch feature:

1. Open your Microsoft Word document (or PDF) with the content you want to transfer into Canva.

2. Open Canva and choose a blank document template.

3. Copy your notes from Word and paste all the text into the new Canva document.

    Alternatively, you can import your document into Canva using the upload button. In this case, I recommend importing the Word content as a `.pdf` file since it has better compatibility.

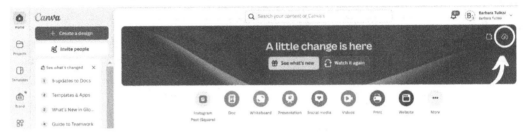

Figure 5.12: The Upload button

4. All the content from your Word document will now be in Canva. Format the content by bolding keywords, using italics on quotes or data, underlining links, using bullet points where needed, and so on. This will help your presentation to be more appealing.

    The formatting only needs to be basic, though – Magic Switch will improve it.

5. In the top menu, click **Magic Switch**, then select **Convert to Presentation**.

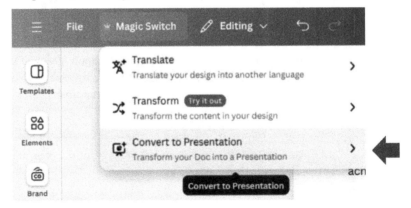

Figure 5.13: The Convert to Presentation feature

6. Canva will display a new screen with some layout suggestions. Select your favorite one.

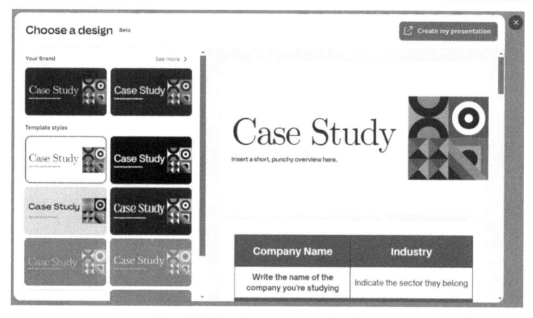

Figure 5.14: Choosing your presentation design

7. Canva will then present your text content as individual slides. Review each slide and make any necessary adjustments. For example, you can rearrange slides, delete unnecessary ones, or even split lengthy slides into separate ones for better flow.

See also

Don't be afraid to experiment with different layouts – we covered them in the *There's more* section of the *Creating a presentation for a client* recipe.

You can also add subtle animations for an extra touch of engagement, which will be covered in a later recipe, *Utilizing animations in your presentation*.

Visualizing data better in your presentations

Let's face it, spreadsheets full of numbers can feel like a flashback to dreaded math tests. Our brains tend to glaze over at endless rows and columns. But here's the truth: data visualization is the key to unlocking the true power of your information. By presenting data in a clear, engaging way, you can not only inform your audience but also inspire them to take action. Think of it as taking your data from the dungeon of dullness and presenting it on a vibrant stage, bathed in the spotlight of clarity and understanding.

In this recipe, you'll become a data visualization wizard, crafting charts and graphs that not only make sense but also leave a lasting impression. So, ditch the numberphobia and get ready to make your data sing beautifully!

Getting ready

In this recipe, we'll use some data that shows the top 10 most widespread waste items polluting oceans. To do this, you can use this spreadsheet that I have prepared for you: `https://docs.google.com/spreadsheets/d/1OMDOLFRa1VYw912T9l4xzUHRrwpXkQxe_anKFoXYPkk/edit?usp=sharing`.

How to do it...

To import your data directly into Canva, follow these steps:

1. Open your Canva presentation project. In the left-hand menu, open the **Elements** panel, then scroll down and find the **Charts** section.

2. A variety of chart types will appear. Select the chart that best suits your data. For our data on the top 10 most widespread waste items polluting oceans, a stacked row chart would be a great choice.

Figure 5.15: The Chart tab

3. Now, instead of manually entering data points, click the **Data** tab at the top of the chart editor window. From there, choose from the following options:

    · **Import data** if you are using a Google spreadsheet such as the one provided in the *Getting ready* section (you may be asked to connect to your Google account).

    · **Upload from file** if you are using data from another source, such as Microsoft Excel.

4. Once you're done, Canva will automatically populate your chosen chart with your data. Now you can do the following:

    · Play around with colors and fonts to customize your graph according to the look and feel of your presentation.

    · Add clear and concise labels to your chart's axes and a title that grabs attention, for example, `10 most widespread waste items polluting oceans`. Keep in mind that short and catchy text is an opportunity for you to help your graph's storytelling.

    · Find an impactful image to put as a background that reinforces your data's message, such as a photo of a plastic-filled ocean.

    This is what I have done:

Figure 5.16: Our pollution chart

5. Once your data visualization masterpiece is complete, click **Save**. Your newly created chart will be available as an element within your Canva project. Simply drag and drop it onto your presentation slide for seamless integration.

Using infographics in your presentations

The previous recipe, *Visualizing data better in your presentations*, focused on graphs and charts. These are the workhorses of data visualization and are ideal for trends, comparisons, and relationships between different entities.

However, in this recipe, we will focus on infographics. Think of infographics as the superheroes of the presentation world. They combine text, data, and visuals into one stunning package, which tells a clear story and maintains the viewer's attention.

But fear not! Even without a cape and mask, you can become an infographic whiz with the power of Canva. By the end of this recipe, you'll be able to take complex information and whip it into visually engaging infographics that not only inform but also inspire.

How to do it...

Suppose you want an infographic in a blog post to explain how to be more creative in your daily routine. You decide that the best way to convey this information is in six easy-to-follow steps. For that, we can use a timeline format – this format perfectly illustrates daily routines, work experiences over time, or any sequence of chronological events that can be numbered:

1. Navigate to Canva's home page and search for `Infographic` in the search bar.
2. Browse Canva's pre-designed infographic templates, looking for a timeline or process-oriented layout that aligns with your content.

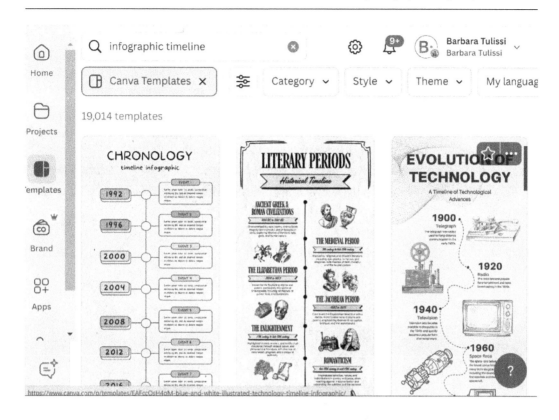

Figure 5.17: Searching for an infographic template

3. Once you've selected a template, start customizing it to match your brand aesthetic:

    *   Use Canva's Brand Kit (if you are using Canva Pro) to ensure consistency with your brand colors, fonts, and logo
    *   If you are using Canva Free, you can copy and paste the hexadecimal colors from your mood board

4. Moving to the infographic itself, replace the placeholder text with the six steps involved in boosting creativity. Ensure to be concise, avoiding jargon and technical terms, to make the steps as clear and easy to follow as possible.

5. Use the **Elements** section to add images, ensuring they are relevant to the steps.

6. Adjust the spacing between the timeline steps for visual harmony. Canva's alignment tools can assist in maintaining a balanced layout. To do so, select all the text boxes; then, in the top menu, select **Position**, go to **Space evenly**, and choose **Vertically**.

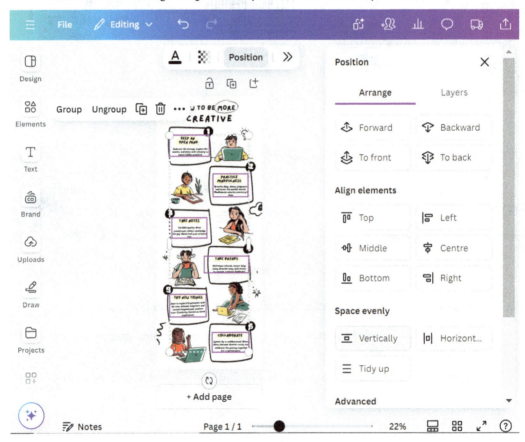

Figure 5.18: The Position menu in Canva

Here is a closer look at our infographic:

Figure 5.19: Our completed infographic

There's more...

Sometimes, finding the right layout for your infographic can be very tricky, I know. That's why I suggest that you first make up your mind about what information you want to show. Then, use the following table to help you choose an appropriate layout:

Layout	What it is	When to use it
A - Chronological (Timeline)	Shows events in order	Historical timelines, product development stages, steps in a process
B - Comparison (Versus)	Highlights differences or similarities	Comparing two things, such as products, concepts, or ideas
C- List	Presents information in a clear, concise way	Steps, tips, ingredients, or other short, bulleted information
D - Hierarchical (Pyramid)	Visualizes relationships between things	Showing how broad categories break down into specific details
E - Flowchart	Visualizes processes with decision points	Guiding viewers through a journey with choices and steps
F - Geographical (Map)	Showcases data connected to locations	Presenting information about specific places or regions
G - Relationship (Venn Diagram)	Shows overlap between sets of information	Highlighting shared and unique elements between two or more concepts
H - Statistical	Focuses on presenting statistical information	Presenting data using charts, graphs, or other visualizations
I - Creative	Uses unique shapes or structures	Complementing your topic in a visually engaging way

Figure 5.20: Table of possible layouts for your infographic

You can see these layouts illustrated here:

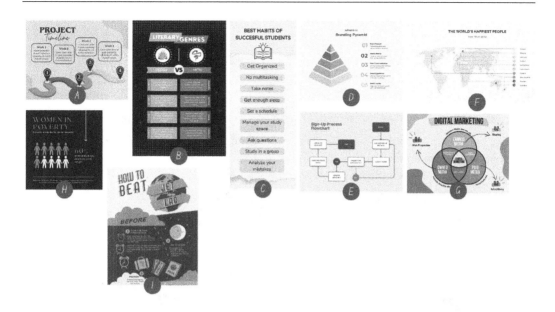

Figure 5.21: Infographic layouts, as described in the previous table

Utilizing animations in your presentations

Animations can be a powerful tool, adding dynamism and visual interest to your slides. Used strategically, they can keep your audience engaged and highlight key points. However, overenthusiastic use of animations can backfire, leaving viewers dizzy and disoriented.

In this recipe, you'll learn how to incorporate animations in three ways – animating pages, animating elements, and adding animations between slides. By the end, you'll be an animation ninja, using them strategically to create captivating and impactful presentations, and you'll feel more confident navigating the world of Canva animations.

Getting ready

Make sure that you have a presentation ready to animate. If you followed along with the *Creating a presentation for a client* recipe, use that one!

How to do it...

As mentioned, Canva offers three main animation approaches:

- Animating pages
- Animating elements
- Adding transition between pages

Let's look at all three approaches.

Page Animations

Page Animations involve animating the entire slide. To do this, follow these steps:

1. Click on the slide you want to animate. Then click the **Animate** button in the top toolbar.

2. Choose an animation style from the **Page Animations** panel, such as **Fade In**, **Zoom In**, or **Bounce**. You can hover over an animation style to see a preview. Once you have chosen one, click on it to apply the animation to your entire slide.

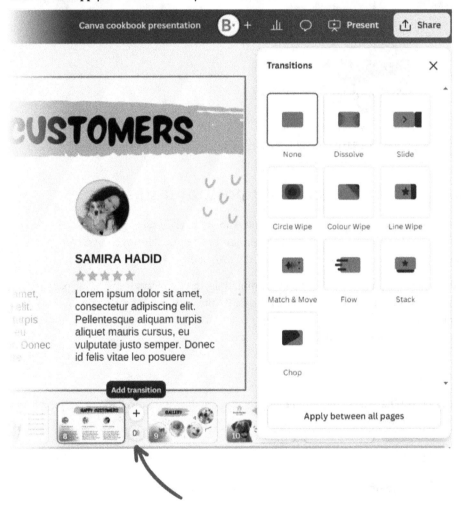

Figure 5.22: Transition between slides feature

3. Some animations give you the possibility to choose between animating **On enter**, **On exit** on **Both**. Choose the option that best fits your situation.

4. You can also customize the duration of the animation using the **Edit time** option in the toolbar, making the animation slower or faster.

Figure 5.23: Animation duration

Element Animations

This option involves adding animations to specific elements. To do this, follow these steps:

1. Click on the element you want to animate on your slide (such as some text, an image, etc.) and then click the **Animate** button in the top toolbar.

2. Navigate to the **Element Animations**, **Photo Animations**, or **Text Animations** sections on the left side panel, where you'll find animations for those elements – this includes **Fly In** for text or **Spin** for images.

3. Similar to animating pages, you can preview animation styles, adjust the duration, and then click to apply the chosen animation to your element.

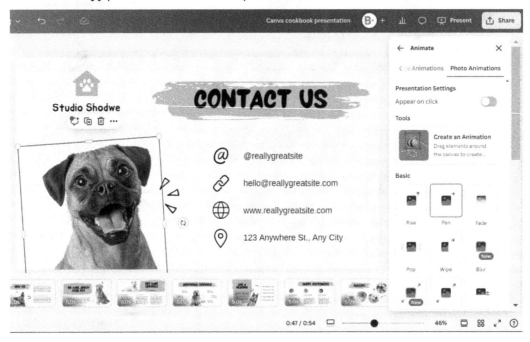

Figure 5.24: Element animation feature

Adding transitions between slides

Adding a transition between one slide and another can make the slide changes more dynamic. It can create the sense of someone turning a page or zooming deeper into a topic – it all depends on the purpose you have and on the transition you choose. Let's see how you can do that:

1. Open the bottom menu to see the slide overview and locate the two slides you want to add a transition between.

2. Hover with your mouse between one slide and another and you will discover two icons: the **Add a new page** icon and the **Add transition** icon.

Figure 5.25: The Add transition icon

3. Click on the **Add transition** icon and you'll see a list of available transition animations. Hover over the options with your mouse to get a preview.

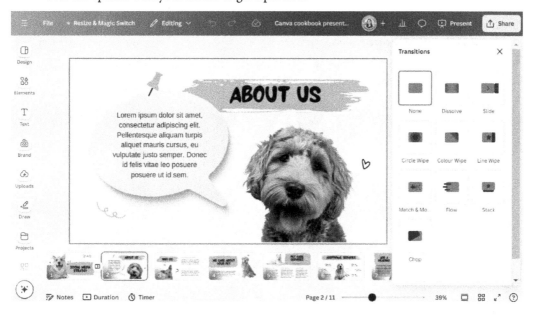

Figure 5.26: Transitions panel

4. The transition menu might offer additional options depending on the chosen effect. This might include a slider or a box to adjust the duration of the animation (how long it lasts). Slide the bar or type in a value (usually between 0.1 and 2.5 seconds) to set your preferred duration.

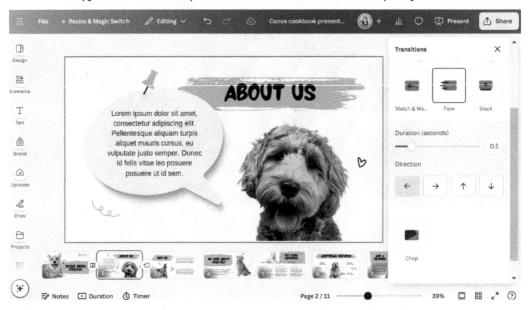

Figure 5.27: Animation options depending on the chosen animation

5. If you want the same transition between all slides, tap the small box next to **Apply between all pages** at the top of the transition menu.

6. To see how your transitions flow, tap the **Present** button in the top right corner, which will allow you to preview your presentation with the added animations.

Figure 5.28: Click Present to see the animation

How it works...

When it comes to animations, here are some dos and don'ts to consider:

Dos	Don'ts
Use animation intentionally. Every animation should serve a purpose. Emphasize key points, reveal information step-by-step, or guide the audience's eye with an animation.	Don't overdo it! Too many animations can overwhelm your audience and distract from your message.
Keep animations subtle and tasteful. Avoid anything flashy or jarring.	Don't animate everything! Not every element on your slide needs to move. Prioritize what benefits from animation.
Maintain consistency, using a similar animation style throughout the presentation for a cohesive feel.	Don't use distracting animations! Avoid animations with sound effects, jarring movements, or excessive flashing.
Control timings, aiming for a comfortable pace that allows the audience to absorb the information. They shouldn't be too slow or too fast.	Don't forget about your audience! Tailor your animations to the context and your audience's expectations. A business presentation might call for a more conservative approach than a creative pitch.

Dos	Don'ts
Preview your presentation to ensure animations flow smoothly and don't distract from your content.	Don't forget about accessibility! Some viewers may have visual impairments or rely on screen readers that might not work well with animations.

Figure 5.29: Dos and don'ts of using animation in presentations

There's more...

Here are some important considerations to be aware of:

- *Sharing via Link*: Keep in mind that adding animations to your presentation and then sharing it through a link will essentially make it a video file for the viewer. This means they won't have the freedom to skip to the next slide whenever they want – they'll need to stop the video and then click play to advance.

- *Downloading as PDF*: If you download your animated presentation as a PDF, be aware that PDFs are static documents and animations won't be displayed.

And some personal advice – use animations sparingly. If everything on your slide is moving, it becomes difficult for the viewer to focus on any one element. We'll delve deeper into the world of video in a dedicated chapter, but for now, remember – a sprinkle of animation can go a long way, while a downpour can leave your audience, well, soaked with boredom.

Presenting presentations in Canva

You've crafted a masterpiece – a presentation that informs, inspires, and (hopefully) wows your audience – but wait, the journey isn't over yet! This recipe equips you with the secret sauce for delivering your Canva presentation with confidence and finesse.

Whether you're aiming for a polished PDF handout, a captivating recorded presentation with your voice and webcam, or a seamless online meeting where you share your screen – this recipe has you covered. We'll navigate the ins and outs of presentation delivery and, by the end, you'll be a presentation ninja, ready to unleash your message in a way that keeps your audience engaged and wanting more.

So, polish those virtual slides, clear your throat (metaphorically, of course), and get ready to take your presentations to the next level!

How to do it...

There are several ways you can present your presentation in Canva. Of course, it depends on your purpose:

- *Classic PDF*: To share a final, uneditable version of your presentation with a client, export it as a PDF. This format preserves the visual integrity of your design and prevents accidental modifications:

  I.   Click the **Share** button and select **Download** from the drop-down menu.

  II.   Choose **PDF Standard** for digital use of your document or **PDF Print** if you need to print your document. I will explain these in more depth in the *Importing, exporting, and sharing your presentations* recipe.

Figure 5.30: Export using PDF options

- *Full-Screen Mode*: For a more immersive experience, present your slides in full-screen mode. To access the full-screen presentation, click on **Present** and choose the first option, **Present full screen**. Then, navigate through your presentation by tapping on the right or left arrows. The mouse cursor will be more visible, making it easier to highlight key points during your screen-sharing presentation.

Figure 5.31: What a full-screen presentation looks like

- *Engage Recording*: Canva allows you to record yourself presenting alongside your slides. To do so, follow these steps:

    I.   Click **Present** in the right corner and choose **Record and present**.

    II.   You will be redirected to the recording studio, where you can set up your mic and camera to record yourself while presenting.

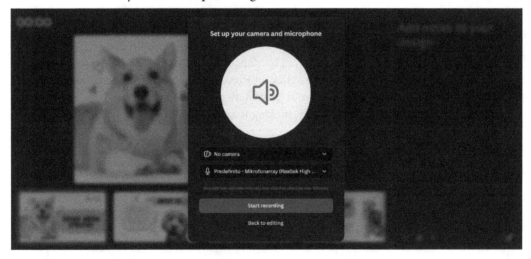

Figure 5.32: Setting up your camera and audio

Then, when you hit **Start recording**, you will see this screen:

Figure 5.33: How to record in Canva

- *Presenter Screen Sharing*: Presenting during online meetings can be very tough, especially if you have a memory like Dory from Finding Nemo. To make this easier, try the following:

I.   To add notes to your slides, click on the **Notes** section below the slide content. This area is private and won't be visible to your audience during the presentation. Use it to jot down key points, reminders, or even the entire script if needed.

Figure 5.34: Showing notes in Canva

II.   Then use the presenter view option to share your screen during online meetings. This way, Canva will create two browser tabs for you:

- One tab that the audience can see:

Figure 5.35: What the audience sees

- And another tab that only you can see, where your notes also appear:

Figure 5.36: What you can see

Of course, if you feel more confident, you can also avoid this option and directly use screen sharing.

- *Animation Magic*: Canva's animation tools add a touch of pizzazz and help maintain your audience's attention. Use the following shortcuts while presenting to unlock their potential:

Shortcut	Effect	Use it when...
B	Blur the screen	You want to create mystery (viewers will be asking themselves, what's on the slide?!)
C	Confetti exploding on your slide	It's time to celebrate something
M	Microphone drop	You end your presentation and feel it was a triumph
O	Floating bubbles	You want viewers to think about something
U	Opening and closing curtains (like a theatre stage)	You're at the beginning or at the end of the presentation
0123456789	Activate a 10-minute countdown	You need to time your speech
Q	Quiet	You need your audience to stay quiet
D	Drumroll	You need to introduce something/someone very important

Figure 5.37: Presentation shortcuts

You can see these animations in the following image too:

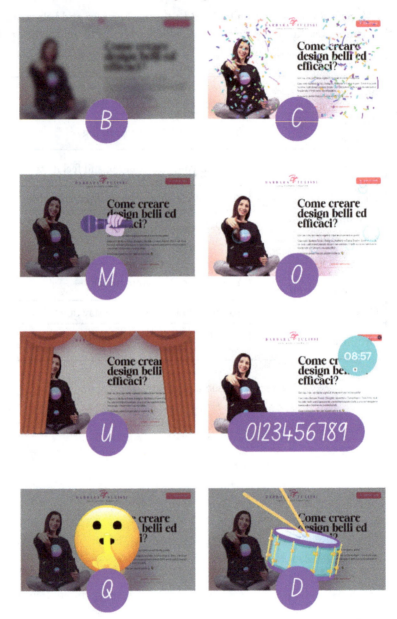

Figure 5.38: Animations in action

There's more...

Outside of Canva, here are some bonus tips to elevate your presentation delivery:

- Rehearse your presentation beforehand, paying attention to timing and pacing

- Speak clearly and with enthusiasm – even when presenting virtually

- Ask questions, use polls (if your meeting platform allows), and encourage interaction to keep everyone involved

By mastering these presentation delivery techniques and leveraging Canva's versatile features, you'll transform your presentations from static slides into captivating experiences that resonate with your audience. So, take a deep breath, unleash your inner presenter, and get ready to show the world what you've created!

Importing, exporting, and sharing your presentations

Ready to share your Canva masterpiece? This guide will walk you through the simple process of importing existing presentations, exporting your finished design, and sharing it with the world. From conference rooms to online platforms, we've got you covered. Let's dive in!

Getting ready

Make sure that you have a presentation ready to animate. If you followed along with the *Creating a presentation for a client* recipe, use that one!

How to do it...

You may find yourself in one of these situations:

- You need to import a presentation from Google Slide or PowerPoint into Canva to utilize Canva's editing tools

- You need to export a Canva presentation into another format

- You want to share a presentation with your client or teammates

Let's dig into these cases!

Importing presentations into Canva

To import a presentation into Canva, follow these steps:

1. In the Canva dashboard, click the upload button (previously shown in *Figure 5.12*).

2. A window will pop up, allowing you to drag and drop your presentation file (`.pdf`, `.pptx`, etc.) directly from your computer.

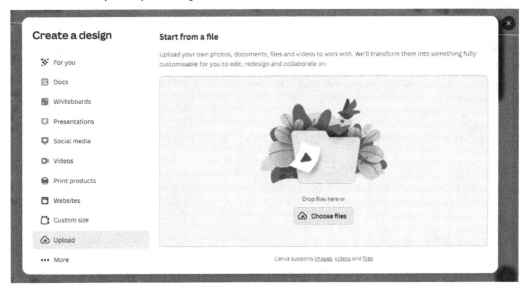

Figure 5.39: Upload popup

Canva is pretty darn clever when it comes to interpreting your imported presentation. It will analyze the file, identifying headings, subheadings, and paragraphs, and convert them into individual Canva slides. This forms the basic structure for your presentation within Canva.

It's important to note that, sometimes, when importing presentations from other programs, especially text-heavy ones, there might be minor formatting hiccups. Text boxes might not translate perfectly, or line breaks could appear in unexpected places. Fear not! Canva allows you to easily adjust them:

I.   Click on the text box with the formatting issue.

II.   Utilize the text editing tools in the top toolbar to adjust font size, style, and alignment.

III.   Break up lengthy text blocks into smaller, more digestible chunks for better readability.

3. With your presentation imported and any formatting issues addressed, you're ready to unleash your creativity! Canva offers a vast library of design elements, allowing you to add visuals, customize backgrounds, and personalize your presentation to truly stand out.

Exporting presentations from Canva

Canva offers a variety of export options to suit your needs:

- **Download as PDF Standard**: This format is perfect for sharing your presentation electronically. It creates a crisp, clear document that retains the overall layout and design of your slides. This is ideal for email attachments or online uploads.

- **Download as PDF Print**: This option creates a high-quality PDF, which is an ideal format for printing. It ensures your presentation looks its best on paper, with clear text and a CMYK color profile.

Figure 5.40: finding the CMYK option for printing colors

- **PPTX**: Canva understands the corporate world still heavily relies on PowerPoint. That's why it allows you to export your presentations as .pptx files (PowerPoint format). This is especially helpful if you're creating presentation templates for speakers at events you organize.

  Within the **Share** drop-down menu, navigate to **Download** and select **PowerPoint (.pptx)**. Canva will export your presentation, allowing speakers to customize it further using their preferred presentation software.

Figure 5.41: Download as PPTX

> **Note**
>
> While Canva offers a vast library of fonts and design elements, it's important to note that PowerPoint might not have all the same fonts. Additionally, some images within your presentation might need to be re-imported when opening the .pptx file in PowerPoint or Google Slides. This is a minor hurdle, and a quick heads-up for your speakers if you choose to export in .pptx format.

Sharing presentations in Canva

Sharing your presentation is as easy as clicking a button! Navigate to the top right corner and click the familiar **Share** button. A drop-down menu will appear, revealing the key to sharing mastery.

Canva empowers you to control who can access your presentation:

- **Share with a specific email address**: This means that the person with that address can edit, comment on, or just view the presentation, depending on what you choose. Canva also provides the possibility to add a private message that the receiver will get via email with the invitation to take a look at the project.

Figure 5.42: Share with a specific email addresses

- **Share via link**: Canva offers you multiple choices about how to share your presentation with your team or clients. You can set the permission as follows:

  - **Anyone with the link can edit**: You can use this if you want to collaborate on that project with lots of different people, such as a copywriter, a social media manager, or another designer. However, because everyone can edit the presentation, I recommend you make a safety copy of your project before sharing it. You can do that by going to **File** and choosing **Create a copy** – this will create a duplicate of your presentation in your Canva dashboard.

  - **Anyone with the link can view**: I personally use this permission when I share my CV or portfolio with companies or clients, so they do not need to download a PDF file to see my works – they will just need to click the link I shared. It also does not matter if they do not have a Canva account; they can access my presentation anyway without the possibility of editing or commenting, of course. This share option is very useful because it's like creating a mini website or media kit with its own URL from which everyone with the link can access.

- **Anyone with the link can comment**: You can use this permission when you just want your team or client to add some comments on it without touching the design or the content.

Figure 5.43: Anyone with the link options

Crafting Captivating Videos

Living in paradise (Gran Canaria, baby!) has its downsides. Sure, the beaches are stunning, but the local wildlife? Not so much. I'm talking about the cucarachas! These speedy demons are basically cockroaches on nitrous oxide. So, picture this: I'm peacefully working at my desk, eyes glued to the computer screen, when suddenly a blur shoots across the floor three meters away. Me? I launch myself onto the sofa like a startled cat, shrieking like a banshee.

What's the point of this story? Well, movement grabs our attention. Especially in a boring, static environment such as my office. That's why, when it comes to creating content, videos rule! Movement is built into us, so our eyes (and our attention) crave it. See where I'm going with this? Videos can be your secret weapon in the daily social media attention war.

That's exactly why TikTok exploded onto the scene – it's a constant stream of movement, a never-ending game of "catch my attention!" But here's the thing: grabbing attention is just the first step. Once you have those eyes glued to your screen, you need to keep them engaged. That's where this chapter comes in.

In this chapter, we'll delve into the art and science of creating videos that truly connect. You'll learn how to harness the power of storytelling, visuals, and animation to produce content that not only stops the scrolling but also inspires action. From conceptualizing your video's purpose to mastering the technical aspects of video creation, we'll cover it all.

We'll also explore essential video elements such as subtitles, GIFs, and highlight creation. Plus, we'll uncover the potential of Canva's AI tools to streamline your video production process.

Ready to transform your video content from ordinary to extraordinary? Let's go!

In this chapter, we will cover the following recipes:

- Defining your video's purpose and message (part 1)

- Structuring and creating your video (part 2)

- Animating your video (part 3)

- Generating subtitles

- Creating GIFs

- Creating a label in Canva and CapCut

- Editing videos with Canva's AI

> **Note**
>
> The first three recipes will guide you through the essential steps of video creation: defining your video's purpose and message, structuring your content effectively, and bringing your vision to life with engaging animations. These elements work in harmony to create videos that captivate your audience and drive results. Therefore, ensure to read them before jumping to the next recipes.

Defining your video's purpose and message (part 1)

Before we jump into the fun stuff with Canva, let's take a quick pit stop to define your video's purpose and message. Every great video starts with a clear goal – what do you want your viewers to walk away thinking/knowing/doing? Once you have that answer, you can focus on crafting visuals and a narrative that truly resonates.

Here, we'll here a look at some handy exercises to help your mind become laser-focused before diving into creation mode, and then look at how to add your notes into Canva.

How to do it...

As mentioned, let's take a look at some exercises. The first two will help you focus on your video's purpose, and the next three will help you consider how to express your video's message.

Here are some focus exercises for your purpose:

1. Imagine you have 30 seconds to explain your video to someone in an elevator. What's the one key takeaway you want them to remember? This quick exercise forces you to focus on the core message and sets a strong foundation for crafting compelling visuals and a clear narrative in your video.

2.   Imagine you have a newspaper headline announcing your video. What's the concise, attention-grabbing statement that captures the essence of your message? This exercise forces you to condense your video's purpose into a single, powerful sentence, ensuring your visuals and narrative all support that core idea.

These exercises show you how to better express your message:

1.   Think about the challenge or pain point your video will address. Then, craft a concise statement outlining the solution your video offers. This approach ensures your video has a clear purpose – to guide viewers from a problem they face to the solution you provide. By focusing on this framework, you can ensure your visuals and narrative directly address the viewer's need and showcase the value your video delivers.

2.   Instead of focusing on pure information, consider the emotional response you want to evoke in viewers. Do you want to inspire them, make them laugh, or leave them feeling empowered? Once you identify the desired emotional impact, craft your message to resonate with that feeling. This approach encourages you to think beyond just facts and figures, and instead focus on how your video will make viewers feel. By keeping this emotional connection in mind, you can tailor your visuals and narrative to truly resonate with your audience.

3.   Imagine your ideal viewer has watched your video. What do you want them to do differently after experiencing it? By envisioning the desired behavior change, you can refine your message to directly address the steps needed to get there. This approach ensures your video has a clear call to action, guiding viewers from simply watching to taking a concrete step toward the solution you offer. Keeping this future vision in mind will help you develop impactful visuals and a narrative that compels viewers to act.

For this recipe, let's imagine we are crafting a video in Canva for a yoga academy. The message must be clear – we need to educate people about yoga benefits – so our elevator pitch might be something like this:

"Feeling overwhelmed by deadlines and to-do lists? Smart workers like you know focus is key. But what if your secret weapon wasn't coffee, but yoga? At Yoga Academy, we help high performers like yourself de-stress, boost energy, and sharpen their focus. Imagine – improved sleep, better posture, and a calmer mind to tackle any challenge. Ready to unlock your peak potential? Let's chat about how yoga can supercharge your workday."

My newspaper headline would be the following:

"Beyond the desk: Yoga Academy empowers smart workers for peak performance."

With that, let's add our notes into Canva so we don't forget them! To do this, follow these steps:

1. Open your Canva dashboard and click the **Video** button:

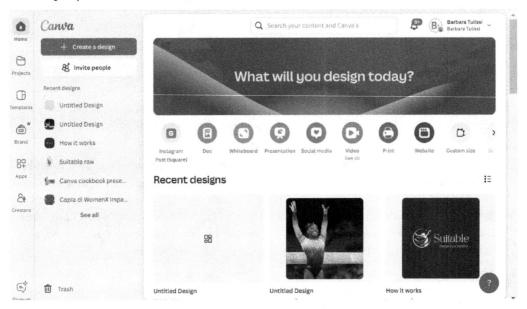

Figure 6.1: Finding the Video section

2. Here, choose the **Mobile Video** format (which measures 1,080x1,920 px):

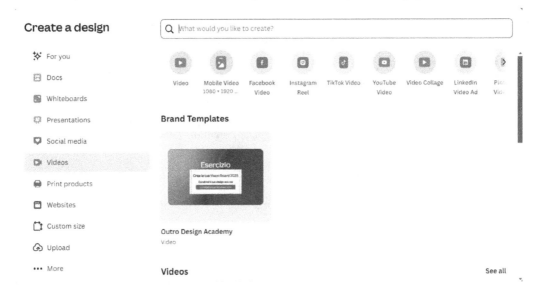

Figure 6.2: Video options

3. Once you are in, click the **Notes** button in the bottom-left corner of the video editor. Then, take our Yoga Academy elevator pitch, as if it could be our video script, and paste it in the first frame's note:

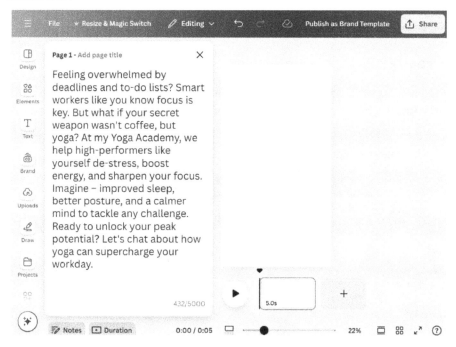

Figure 6.3: Canva's note section

There's more...

Video notes are like a secret weapon for planning your text. Here's why:

- Use the notes to jot down the text for each frame, like a mini-script. This gives you a bird's-eye view of your entire video's flow.

- Use the notes to figure out how much text goes in each frame. This helps avoid overloading viewers with too much text at once.

- Is a frame overflowing with text? The notes help you decide whether you need to lengthen that frame or split it into multiple frames, ensuring viewers have enough time to read comfortably.

Basically, the **Notes** section acts as a hidden storyboard for your text, helping you craft a smooth and engaging video experience.

Now that we have defined our purpose (promoting Yoga Academy) and our message (the one in the script), let's jump into the next recipe: *Structuring and creating your video (part 2)*.

Structuring and creating your video (part 2)

Now that we've nailed our Yoga Academy video's purpose and message (high five!), let's dive into defining the structure. Here, we'll craft a clear roadmap for your video, ensuring your message flows seamlessly and keeps viewers engaged. Then, we'll start actually creating it!

Getting ready

We will continue using the Yoga Academy example introduced in *Defining your video's purpose and message*. Make sure you have a video open in Canva, with the dimensions 1,080x1,920 px.

Looking back at *Figure 6.3*, we can see our video's script is too long to stay in a single frame, so we have to divide it into more frames along the timeline:

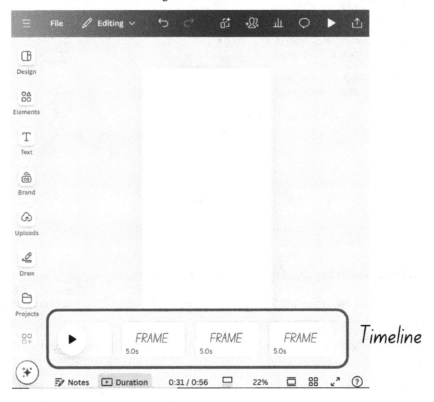

Figure 6.4: Canva's timeline and frames

To do this, instead of having the script on one frame, split the text across six frames instead, like so:

- *Frames 1 and 2 – the problem*: Feeling overwhelmed by deadlines and to-do lists? and Smart workers like you know focus is key.

Figure 6.5: First and second frames' notes

- *Frame 3 – the solution*: But what if your secret weapon wasn't coffee, but yoga?

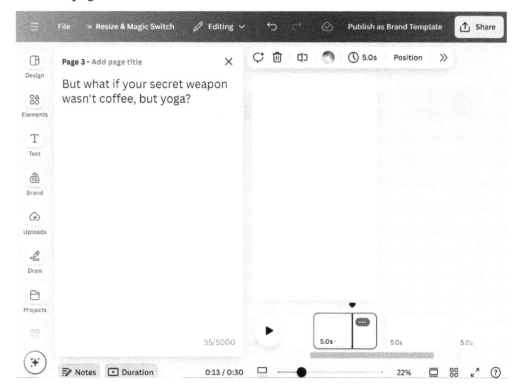

Figure 6.6: Third frame's note

- *Frames 4 and 5 – highlight the benefits*: `At Yoga Academy, we help high-performers like yourself de-stress, boost energy, and sharpen their focus and Imagine – improved sleep, better posture, and a calmer mind to tackle any challenge.`

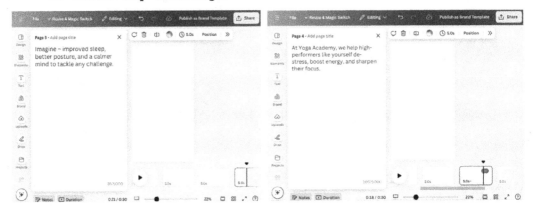

Figure 6.7: Fourth and fifth frames' notes

- *Frame 6 – call to action*: `Ready to unlock your peak potential? Let's chat about how yoga can supercharge your workday.`

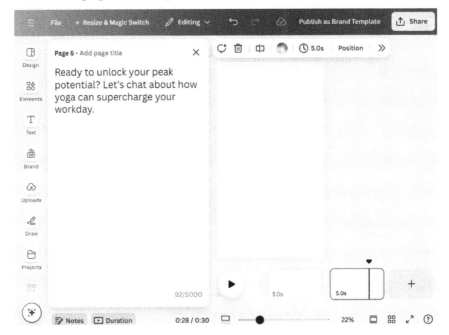

Figure 6.8: Sixth frame's note

How to do it...

Now that you have the clear structure, let's start to craft our video in Canva:

1. Let's start by working on the first frame:

    I.   From the left-hand menu, open the **Elements** options and select **Video**.

    II. In the search bar, search for something such as `yoga studio`. We want to find a video of a serene atmosphere or a person practicing a relaxing pose.

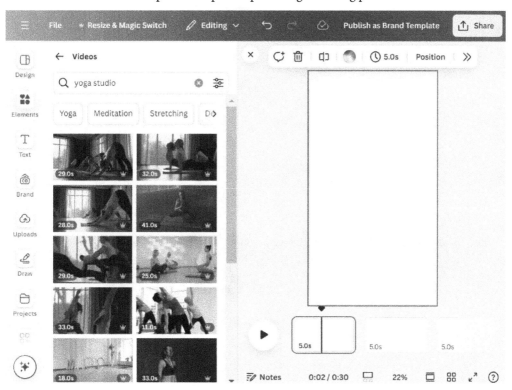

Figure 6.9: Customizing the first frame

    III. Select your favorite video to add it to your design, then right-click on it and choose **Set as a background**.

    IV. Now, add our first frame's script. Open up the **Notes** section, copy and paste the text, add a textbox (use the *T* shortcut), and replace the placeholder text with our first frame's script.

V.   It can be useful to apply a background effect under text to improve legibility. To do so, select the textbox, click **Effects** on the toolbar, then select the background effect. Play around with the color and the border sharpness to find the perfect fit.

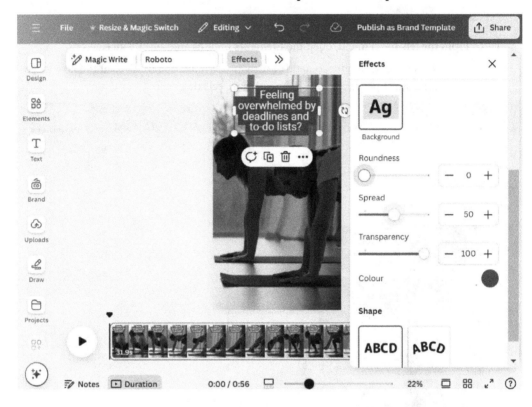

Figure 6.10: Applying the text background effect

VI.   Further customize it with your brand identity, fonts, and colors.

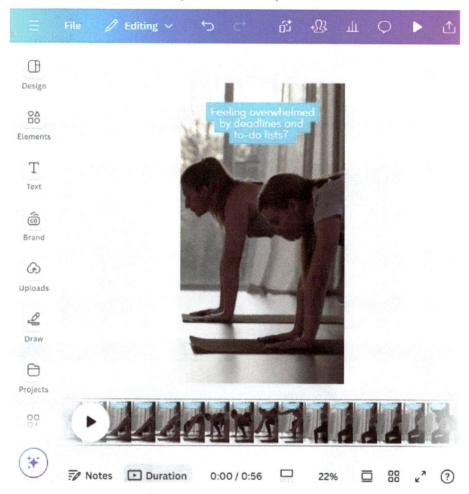

Figure 6.11: Applying your fonts and colors to the first frame

2. Now, let's move on to frames 2, 3, 4, and 5. For each frame, select the frame from the timeline and then follow these steps:

   I.   In the **Elements** | **Video** tab, find a yoga-related video and set it as the background.

   II.   Add a textbox using *T* and paste the frame's note text inside.

   III. Apply a background effect beneath the text for improved legibility.

   IV.   Customize the frame with your brand identity, font, and colors.

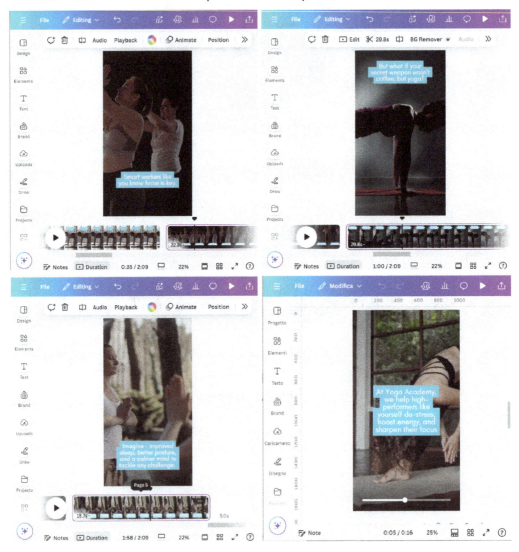

Figure 6.12: Crafting frames 2 to 5

3. The last frame is usually different from the others, as here you want to lead the viewer to do something (the call to action):

    I.   As before, from the **Elements | Video** tab, find a yoga-related video and set it as the background.

    II. Add a textbox (*T*) with the final portion of the script, along with a text background for legibility, and your brand identity.

    III. Now, back in the **Elements** tab, search for button, and look for an animated button that you will add to your design. Customize the button with the colors of your brand and place it under the previous textbox. Create another textbox, add CONTACT US inside it, and place it above the button.

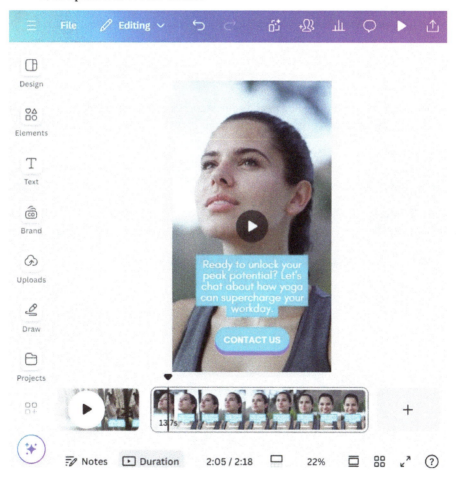

Figure 6.13: Crafting the sixth frame

Now that we've crafted a visually stunning design, it's time to add the finishing touch: animation! Let's transform your static video into a dynamic masterpiece. Follow along with the next recipe!

Animating your video (part 3)

Now that we've tackled the purpose and message of our Yoga Academy video and structured and created it, let's bring the video to life! In this recipe, I'll guide you through animating your designs directly in Canva. We'll transform static elements into dynamic visuals, creating an engaging experience for your audience.

Getting ready

Make sure you have your Yoga Academy video from the *Structuring and creating your video (part 2)* recipe.

How to do it...

In the following subsections, we are going to add some animations and transitions, set frame timing, add music, and preview our video to export it in the end.

Adding animations

To start, let's add some animation to our frames:

1. For the first frame, since we already have an animated background, we can add a soft text animation. As this is the introductory frame, a fade effect would be appropriate:

    I.   Select the text and choose **Animate** from the toolbar.

    II.   From the **Animate** panel, choose **Fade**, as well as **On enter**. You can also adjust the animation speed if you like.

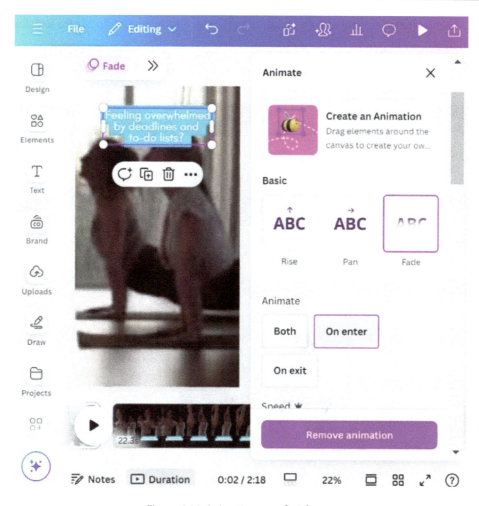

Figure 6.14: Animating your first frame

2. For the second, third, fourth, and fifth frames, we have set videos as background. Canva allows you to animate images and videos, so let's apply an animation to our dynamic backgrounds!

    I.   Select the frame's background and, in the toolbar, click the **Animate** option.

    II. Search for the **Photo Flow** animation. For a yoga business, animated backgrounds can evoke a sense of tranquility and relaxation. To achieve this, consider using subtle, nature-inspired animations that appear as soon as the slide loads. Plus, by avoiding exit animations, you maintain a smooth visual flow between slides.

3. To animate the call to action frame, we can add a transition between the fifth and the sixth frame:

    I. In the timeline, hover your mouse on the blank space between frame 5 and frame 6. Two icons will show up – the first one (the + icon) allows you to add a frame in between, and the second one (the one that looks like >) allows you to add a transition. Click the > icon.

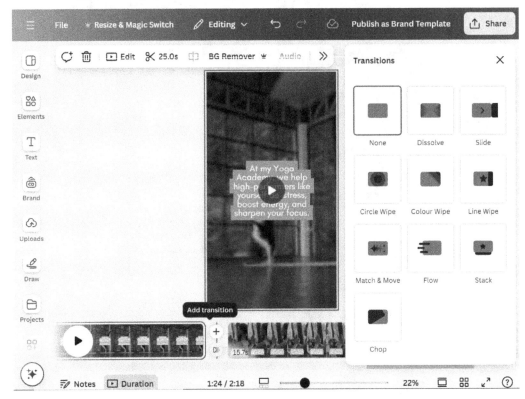

Figure 6.15: Finding the transition option

II.   From the **Transitions** panel, choose the **Match & Move** animation and reduce its speed
for a smoother effect.

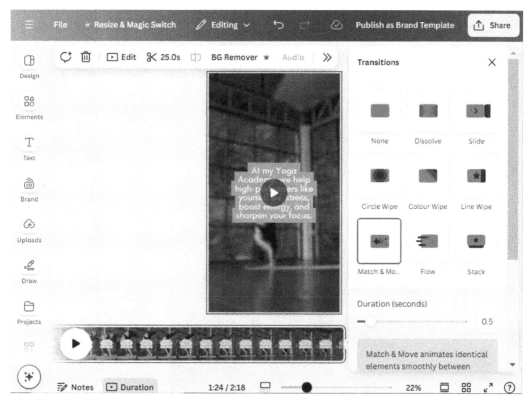

Figure 6.16: Adding transitions

Setting timings

When crafting a video with text overlays, setting the right duration for each frame is crucial. We want
viewers to absorb the information, not get whiplash trying to keep up! To set the timings, follow
these steps:

1.   Access the timeline by either of the following methods:

    •   Selecting the frame's background to set the frame's duration

    •   Selecting specific textboxes or objects within the frame to set their durations

    In this case, we want to set the timing of the frames.

2. Look for the **Trim** option (the *scissors* icon). Clicking it lets you define a custom duration for that selected frame. Let's set the following:

- Frame 1 to 2.5 seconds

- Frames 2, 3, 4, and 5 to 1.5 seconds

- Frame 6 to 3 seconds (since this is the ending, we want the viewer to have sufficient time to read the call to action)

Figure 6.17: Setting timings

3. Now, press the **Play** button. Watch the video with fresh eyes, pretending you've never seen it before. Does the pacing feel natural? Do you have enough time to read all the text? These questions will help you adjust any durations further.

Adding music

Your Yoga Academy video is visually stunning with its animations, but let's add the magic ingredient: a captivating soundtrack!

Hold on a second, though. If you plan to post your video on Instagram, Facebook, TikTok, or YouTube, it's actually better to export the video without music first. You can then add your own commercial music or royalty-free music directly on those platforms to avoid potential copyright issues after any recent updates to their music policies.

So, here's how to seamlessly integrate music into your Canva video:

1. Navigate to the left-hand menu and open **Elements**. Then, in the **Audio** tab, find the audio you like the most, such as some relaxing yoga music. You can preview the audio by clicking on it.

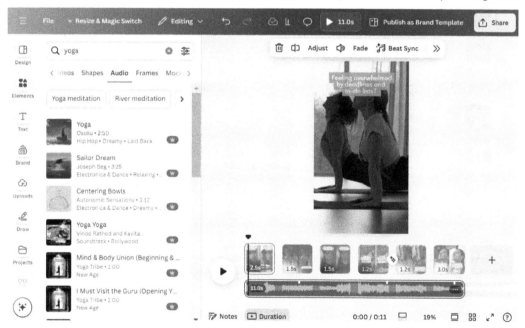

Figure 6.18: Adding music

> **Note**
> You could also upload an `.mp3` file (of a voiceover, for example) and select it from the **Audio** tab.

2. Once you select your music, a new bar will appear on your video timeline preview. Simply drag and drop the audio onto the timeline and position it where you want the music to start in your video.

3. Next, click on the three dots icon on the audio track, choose **Fade**, and apply a **Fade in** and **Fade out** effect at the beginning and end of the track.

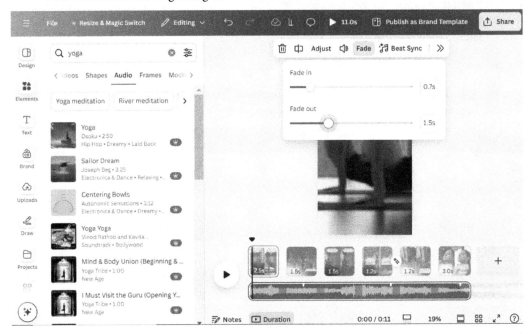

Figure 6.19: Finding music effects

4. Next to the **Fade** option, you can also find the **Volume** option. Change this to your desired volume. My advice is that the music should not distract from the text (nor the voiceover, if you choose to include one).

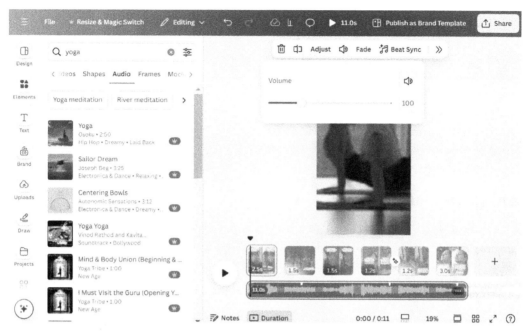

Figure 6.20: Setting the volume

While the free version of Canva offers basic audio editing tools such as trimming and fading in/out options, Canva Pro elevates your video creation experience with the powerful Beat Sync feature.

Beat Sync automatically synchronizes your video content with the rhythm of your chosen soundtrack. This eliminates the tedious process of manual alignment, ensuring a seamless and impactful audio-visual experience for your viewers.

Additionally, Canva Pro allows you to do the following:

- **Fine-tune the music harmony**: Achieve a perfect audio blend by adjusting the music to seamlessly complement your video's narrative

- **Utilize advanced trimming options**: Precisely trim audio sections for a polished final product

Previewing and exporting

Now that your Yoga Academy video is a harmonious blend of visuals, text, and music, it's time to preview your creation and get it ready for the world:

1. To preview your video, press the **Play** button in the Canva editor. This is your chance to check for any timing issues, text readability, or unexpected audio glitches. Pay close attention to the transitions between frames and the overall flow of your video. Does it feel smooth and engaging? Is it moving too fast or do we need to slow the frames down? Does the audio sound good?

2. Once you're happy with your video, click the **Download** button in the top-right corner of the editor. Canva offers a variety of export options depending on your needs. Choose **MP4 video** for the most common and widely compatible format.

> **Tip**
> If you plan to upload your video to social media platforms such as Instagram or Facebook, Canva allows you to choose a specific video resolution during export. Check each platform's recommended video resolution for optimal quality.

Generating subtitles

Ever scroll through social media with the volume off, not wanting to disturb those around you? Maybe you're in a situation where headphones aren't handy. Or maybe you have hearing difficulties and need the post to be more accessible. That's where captions and subtitles come in.

However, while both captions and subtitles provide text overlays for videos, there is a difference:

- **Captions** are automatically generated transcripts that appear when a video is played within the Canva platform. However, these captions are not embedded within the video file itself. As a result, when you download a video with captions from Canva, the captions will not be included. Captions can also not be edited if Canva misinterprets the audio and generates a mistake. You will learn how to add captions to a video in *Chapter 9*.

- **Subtitles**, on the other hand, are manually added text overlays that become part of the video file. These can be generated (and edited!) through Canva's **Subtitles** app. When you download a video with subtitles, the subtitles are embedded, ensuring they are visible on any device or platform where the video is played.

In this recipe, we'll focus on subtitles, showing you how to easily add them to your videos.

How to do it...

To create subtitles in Canva, follow these steps:

1. Start a video project. I love using subtitles for my vertical videos on Instagram and TikTok, so let's use a 1,080x1,920 px format. (Don't worry – subtitles still work on horizontal videos!)

2. Since subtitles only work on videos or audio that have a voice embedded, add a video of you talking in front of the camera, uploading it in the **Upload** section of your project. Then, set it as the video's background.

3. Next, navigate to the **Apps** tab. From there, search for and select **Subtitles**.

4. Once you start the subtitles generation, Canva will take a while to analyze the video. Then, it will show some customization options, such as subtitle style, size, and position. Find the options that best fit.

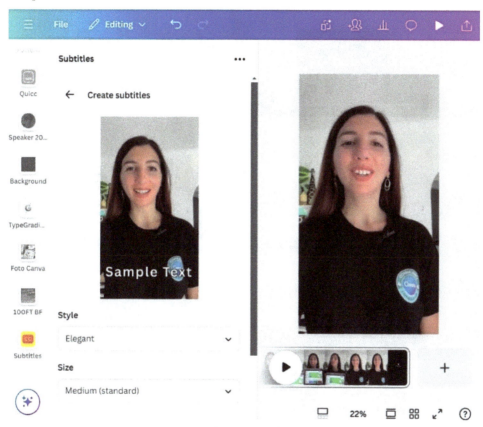

Figure 6.21: Customizing the subtitles

Note

At the moment, Canva can only generate subtitles in English. Hopefully, Canva will be able to provide more languages soon!

5. Now, the app will split your script into editable lines so you can double-check the subtitles or edit your text:

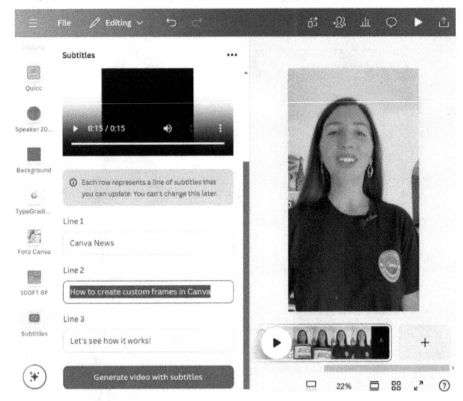

Figure 6.22: Editing the subtitles

6. Click **Generate video with subtitles** and Canva will give you a preview of your subtitled video.

7. Now, it will ask if you want to add the new video with subtitles to your design, replacing the older one. Say yes!

8. When you are done, you can export your video, downloading it as an .mp4 file.

> **Tip**
>
> Consider exporting your video with and without subtitles. This gives you flexibility when sharing your video on different platforms. Some platforms, such as YouTube, allow you to upload captions separately, while others might require embedded subtitles.

> **Note**
>
> The point of this recipe was to review adding captions in Canva, perfect for simple video projects. However, for ultimate customization and advanced editing features, exploring dedicated video editing apps such as CapCut might be the way to go!

Creating GIFs

Forget fleeting video clips – the internet craves bite-sized entertainment that grabs attention in a flash! Enter the glorious GIF: a looping sequence of images, often bursting with humor, that can stop a scroller dead in their tracks. It's not a full video, but rather a way to stitch a series of pictures together, creating a quick and catchy snippet guaranteed to tickle the funny bone.

And what better muse for such hilarity than the eternal kings and queens of the internet? Kittens! In this recipe, we'll be crafting an irresistibly funny GIF starring a fluffy, adorable kitten. Get ready to harness the power of Canva's GIF maker and transform your feline friend's antics into a social media sensation!

How to do it...

To create a GIF, follow these steps:

1. Start a new Canva project. It could have the size of a Facebook or Instagram post depending on where you want to post the GIF once finished.
2. Grab two of your favorite kitten images and upload them to Canva.
3. Place your first kitten picture on the first page of your project and set it as a background.

4. Click on the **Thumbnail view** icon at the bottom of the project interface. Here you will find the **Duration** button. Click on it and look up at the top menu, where you will see the time icon.

Figure 6.23: The first frame of the GIF

5. Set the duration of your first page to 1 second.

6. Add a new page to your project, then set your second kitten picture as the background.

Figure 6.24: The second frame of the GIF

7. Repeat the procedure to set the duration of this second page to 1 second.

8. Now, preview your GIF using the **Play** button.

> **Note**
>
> If I wanted to, I could add more images of my hand, each one moving closer to my eyes, to create a more realistic sense of motion – like a flipbook or stop motion.

9. Once you are done, export your GIF in GIF format and post it on your favorite social media!

You can see my final result here: https://partner.canva.com/4PkdXM.

> **Tip**
> Feeling uninspired by your own cat videos (or maybe your feline overlord isn't feeling particularly comedic today)? No worries! Canva offers a built-in gem – the Giphy app! This handy integration allows you to search and explore a vast library of royalty-free GIFs directly within Canva. There's no need to download them separately – simply find the purrfect GIF that complements your project and add it straight into your design. It's the ultimate shortcut for creating hilarious and engaging content in no time!

Creating a label in Canva and CapCut

In today's digital landscape, creating a consistent brand identity across all platforms is essential. Incorporating recognizable elements, such as your Instagram icon and username, into your YouTube reels can help strengthen your brand's presence and make a lasting impression on viewers.

By including a label in your YouTube reels, you're establishing a visual connection between your YouTube channel and your Instagram profile. This reinforces your brand's identity and encourages viewers to explore your other social media channels. Additionally, a label can help you stand out from the competition and make your reels more memorable.

The label can be created in Canva; however, it's CapCut, a powerful mobile video editing app, that will help bring your label designs to life. By combining the creative power of Canva for label design and the editing capabilities of CapCut, you can create professional-quality video content that effectively engages your audience and leaves a lasting impression. Let's see how!

Getting ready

In this recipe, you will need the following:

- A Canva account, of course
- A CapCut account – which you can sign up for free via `capcut.com`

> **Note**
> If CapCut is not available in your territory, a potential alternative could be InShot (however, these instructions will focus on CapCut).

- A video where you speak in front of the camera

I suggest following this recipe using your phone as, in my opinion, CapCut offers a better experience on mobile than on desktop. Using Canva on your phone will also make it easier to move from Canva to CapCut.

How to do it...

To create our label, we'll start in Canva:

1. Create a new Canva project. I usually use the square 1,080x1,080 px size, but the specific size really isn't important as we will be cropping later.

2. Add a square to your design using the keyboard shortcut *R*. Resize the square to make it longer and slimmer, so it is now a rectangle. Round the corners, and color the rectangle white.

3. Color the page background green. The green background will act later as a reference point for CapCut's chroma-keying feature. This allows you to easily remove the background, allowing the label animation we are going to set up to run smoothly.

4. Next, in the **App** tab, type `Brandfetch`, and open the Brandfetch app.

5. Within the Brandfetch search bar, type `Instagram` and add the Instagram logo to your design.

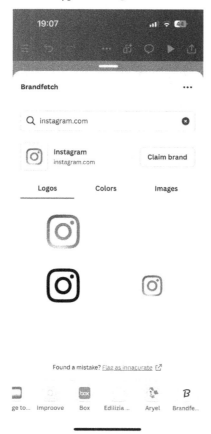

Figure 6.25: Finding the Instagram logo within the Brandfetch app

6. Place the Instagram icon on the left side of the rectangle.

7. Now, double-click on the rectangle to write your Instagram username, then customize it with the font and color you like the most, and align the text to the right of the Instagram icon.

8. Now, let's animate the label:

    I. Select all the elements of your design. You can do it by tapping and holding the first element (for instance, the Instagram icon), clicking the **Select more elements** option, and tapping the other elements. Then, choose the **Group** option.

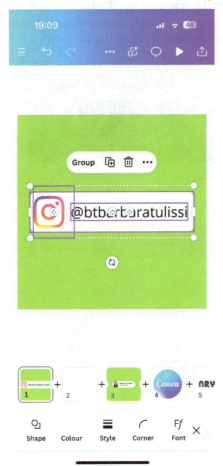

Figure 6.26: Grouping your label's elements

II.   Look for the **Animate** button in the toolbar.

III.   Choose the animation you like the most – in my case, I chose **Blur**.

Figure 6.27: Animating your label

9.   Download your label as an .mp4 file.

Now, let's move to CapCut:

1. Open the CapCut app and import the video of you talking in front of the camera.

2. From the bottom toolbar, scroll until you find **Overlay**. Select it.

3. Choose your downloaded Canva label.

Figure 6.28: Adding your label in CapCut

4. Once added to your video timeline, select your overlay and scroll to find **Remove BG**.

5. Select it, then choose **Chroma key**. The tool will work as an eyedrop – it detects the green color once selected and completely removes it.

Figure 6.29: Removing the label's background in CapCut

Want to check the final result? Let's have a look here: https://drive.google.com/file/d/1D 4eeGbvzpEJswdUGdTCNTvuAyzaoHiPZ/view?usp=sharing.

> **Note**
>
> Always remember to adjust the length of the main video and the overlay to ensure the label shows up at the right time.

Editing videos with Canva's AI

Ever feel like creating captivating video content is an uphill battle against the clock? We've all been there. But what if I told you there's a way to unleash the power of AI to create stunning videos in a flash?

Buckle up because, in this recipe, we're diving headfirst into the magic of Canva's AI video editor!

Getting ready

To follow along, you will need at least three video clips – I will use clips of me talking in front of my mobile camera. You will also need a Canva team subscription but if you do not have one, you can spend your Canva free coins (reserved for AI features only) to try this powerful feature.

How to do it...

To start working with Canva's video AI, follow these steps:

1. Start a new project. I will choose a mobile video format.

2. On the left panel, select the **Design** tab, then select **Generate videos instantly**.

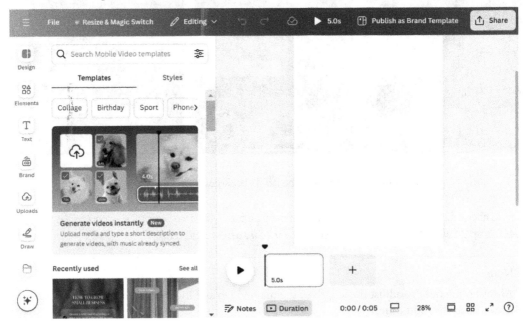

Figure 6.30: Finding the Generate videos instantly button

3. The **Generate video instantly** dialog box appears. Here, upload the clips you wish to use on your video (you could also upload images and other assets if you wish) or simply select already uploaded videos within your library.

4. Then, describe the kind of video you want. Canva will use this to auto-generate and auto-edit a video matching your text prompt. In my case, since I want to craft an educational video, I will type `Education video about Canva`.

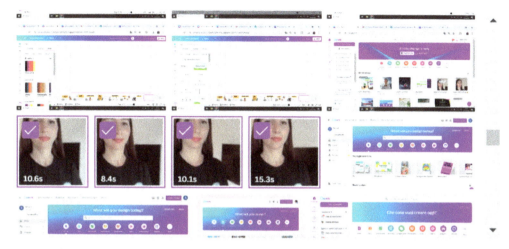

Figure 6.31: Uploading your clips and adding a prompt

5. Click **Generate** and you can preview the generated AI video.

6. Do you like it? Save, download, and share your video project on all your social media accounts directly from Canva.

   Want to see my result? Check it out here: `https://partner.canva.com/EKnj0e`.

> **Note**
>
> While Canva's AI features are continually evolving, keep in mind that they may still have limitations. Be patient as these tools are relatively new and will benefit from user feedback. For now, consider using AI to automate repetitive tasks, such as combining clips. Then, unleash your creativity to personalize and refine the final product.

7
Mastering Eye-Catching, Stop-Scrolling Ads

Imagine scrolling endlessly through your social media feed, a blur of faces, products, and updates. Suddenly, an ad stops you cold. It's visually arresting, the message is clear, and you find yourself wanting to know more. That's the power of a stop-scrolling ad, and in this chapter, I'll equip you to create them yourself using the user-friendly platform Canva.

In this chapter, we'll unravel the secrets of creating ads that truly stand out. From mastering visual design principles to crafting compelling copy and utilizing effective **calls to action** (**CTAs**), you'll gain the knowledge and skills needed to captivate your audience and achieve your marketing goals.

We'll delve into specific techniques, such as optimizing your ads for different platforms, finding inspiration from successful campaigns, and crafting persuasive CTAs. By the end of this chapter, you'll be equipped to transform your ads from ordinary to extraordinary.

Get ready to elevate your ad game and make a lasting impression on your audience.

In this chapter, we will cover the following recipes:

- Defining your ad's objective and target audience
- Finding references to get inspiration
- Tailoring ad formats for different platforms
- Crafting stop-scrolling ads
- Utilizing CTAs effectively

Defining your ad's objective and target audience

Before diving into stunning visuals, let's solidify the foundation of your ad's success. Here, we'll tackle defining your objective: what do you want your ad to achieve? We'll also pinpoint your ideal audience, ensuring your message resonates with exactly the right people. By the end of this section, you'll be crystal clear on your ad's purpose and who you're aiming to reach.

However, hold on a second! Are you sure that you know the difference between ordinary content posted on your brand's social media and an actual ad? Let's clear that up first. While both live on social media, their destinations and goals are distinct:

- **White posts** are content created for your brand's organic social media presence. It aims to build relationships with your audience, foster brand awareness, and spark conversations. Think of it as an invitation to your party – fun, informative, and hopefully leaving a lasting impression. Visually, white posts can be more flexible, incorporating your brand aesthetic while experimenting with trends and formats.

- **Paid social media campaigns**, on the other hand, are targeted ads displayed on platforms such as Facebook or Instagram, as well as Google. These aim for a more direct response, be it driving website traffic, increasing sales, or generating leads. Imagine paid content as a flashy billboard on the way to the party – it needs to be clear, concise, and grab attention quickly. Visually, paid ads often prioritize clean layouts, strong CTAs, and messaging tailored to the specific audience you're targeting.

Now that you get your idea on the way, let's discuss the fact that defining your ad's objective and target audience is so important to get an effective visual impact.

How to do it...

Ideally, in a larger marketing team, defining the ad's objective and target audience falls under the expertise of a media buyer or advertiser. They leverage market data, client goals, and budget constraints to craft a strategic plan. However, in the trenches of solo-preneurship and freelancing, we often wear multiple hats. While a dedicated media buyer optimizes campaigns for maximum impact, understanding these fundamentals empowers you to at least get started.

Think of it this way: a media buyer provides the blueprint, but as a designer, you're the architect who translates that plan into a visually compelling ad. Even without a dedicated media buyer, by grasping the purpose (objective) and target audience, you can tailor your Canva designs with laser focus.

Remember, design isn't just about artistic expression; it's a powerful tool for achieving marketing goals. By understanding these core elements, you'll be well-equipped to collaborate with clients or even take on basic campaign management tasks when needed. This knowledge will make you a more valuable asset, especially when working with clients with limited budgets.

Identify your objective

What do you want your ad to achieve? Here are some common goals:

- **Generating website traffic**: Drive users to a specific landing page showcasing your product or service. (Think website launch or a new blog post!)

- **Increasing brand awareness**: Get your brand name in front of a wider audience. (Ideal for new businesses or product launches.)

- **Boosting sales and conversions**: Encourage direct purchases or sign-ups. (Perfect for e-commerce stores or lead generation campaigns.)

- **Driving app downloads**: Get users to download your mobile app. (Great for showcasing app features.)

Identifying your target audience

Who are you trying to reach? Understanding your ideal customer is key:

- Define demographics such as age, location, interests, and online behavior. You can use a variety of tools to help you, such as the following:

  - **Meta Ads**: Facebook offers powerful audience insights based on user demographics and interests ("likes" and groups).

  - **Google Ads**: Leverage keyword research to identify users actively searching for products or services related to yours.

- Be specific. If you were a marathon-running brand, you wouldn't just target "runners." Refine it to "marathon runners training for their first sub-four race" for a more targeted reach.

- Create buyer personas to visualize your target audience. Sketch out demographics and interests, and even include a moodboard reflecting their visual preferences.

Finding references to get inspiration

Feeling stuck on ad design inspiration? In this section, I'll show you how to find stellar reference materials to jumpstart your creativity. For this, we'll momentarily leave Canva and explore Meta Ads Library, a tool that can help you understand which ads are active on social media platforms and what they have in common.

> **Note**
>
> Of course, Meta Ads Library is not the only tool you can use to find inspiration. You can also browse Pinterest, Instagram, or Canva's **Template** section, as we covered when discussing the "steal like an artist" method in *Chapter 4*.

We will also deal with some strategic insights that I think are crucial to really grabbing your audience's attention.

How to do it...

Let's first unveil what the Meta Ads Library is and how it works and then cover some strategic insight for you. Ready?

Meta Ads Library

To utilize the Meta Ads Library:

1. Head over to Meta's Ads Library (`https://www.facebook.com/ads/library/`). Here, you can peek at what your competitors are doing, giving you insights into high-performing creatives and layouts. By spying (ethically, of course!), you can gather valuable inspiration for crafting captivating Meta ads in Canva. It allows you to search for ads currently running on Facebook and Instagram based on various criteria, including the following:

    *   **Advertiser**: Enter your competitor's name to see all their active ads

    *   **Location**: Filter by region to understand what resonates in your target audience's location

    *   **Keywords**: Search for keywords related to your product/service and see what visuals competitors use

2. Analyze what grabs your attention, paying attention to elements in the ads that stand out:

    *   **Visuals**: Are they using images, videos, or carousels? What kind of imagery resonates (lifestyle shots, product close-ups, explainer videos)?

    *   **Copywriting**: What messaging grabs your attention? Do they focus on benefits, emotions, or humor?

    *   **CTA**: How are they prompting users to engage? Do they use terms such as **Shop Now**, **Learn More**, and **Download**, which send a clear message?

3. Identify commonalities (but don't copy them!). Look for patterns across your competitor's ads. Are there specific design elements, color palettes, or messaging styles consistently present? This can give you clues about what's resonating with their audience, and therefore what can resonate with yours.

4. Grab your references. I'm literally a screenshot addict, so when I see something interesting, I screenshot it and upload it to Canva's cloud, so I'm sure it's safe from my deletion fits! Therefore, I advise you to do the same with the projects that you find most interesting and add them in Canva so you can reference them before starting to create your project.

5. Once you've crafted your ad based on competitor insights and your own creativity, consider A/B testing different versions. A/B test consists of creating multiple versions of your ad (changing, for example, a color or a text within your design) and tracking its performance, allowing you to make data-driven decisions to improve your campaigns.

> **Note**
>
> Of course, A/B testing is not work for a designer or social media manager, but as I like to contribute strategically to my client's projects, I always create more than one version of the same design to be tested.

Strategic insights

Here's the ultimate ingredients list to craft an effective ad that grabs your audience's attention (hey, take note!). Take a look at what your competitors are doing in Meta Ad Library. Here, you'll observe some common patterns in successful ads:

- **Headline hero**: A clear, concise headline should give your viewer an immediate idea of what your ad is all about.

- **Focus on visuals:** While video can be powerful, static images are still widely used. Make sure the visuals are related to the topic/ad.

- **Humanizing your ad**: Consider using your picture or the course coach's image instead of generic visuals. People are naturally drawn to human faces – their eyes and expressions can grab attention more effectively than stock photos. This is especially true if they've already encountered you through other courses, building brand recognition.

- **Engaging content**: While maintaining attention is key, go beyond a simple headline. Consider adding the following:

  - **Cost**: Clearly communicate the course price upfront

  - **Limited availability**: Create a sense of urgency by mentioning limited spots

  - **Social proof**: Provide positive testimonials to build trust

- **Tangible representation**: Selling an online course? Design a mockup box to represent it as a physical product. This can trigger a sense of tangibility, making it easier for viewers to imagine owning and using the course.

- **Clarity is crucial**: Don't overwhelm viewers with text overload! Keep information concise and benefit-oriented to maintain focus. Remember, the goal is to strike a balance between grabbing attention and providing valuable information.

- **CTA power**: Don't leave users wondering what to do next – a prominent call-to-action button (like **Learn more**) is a must-have!

Figure 7.1: Anatomy of a performing ad

> **Tip**
>
> Don't just limit yourself to the Meta Ads Library. Look at competitor websites, social media pages, and even industry publications for additional design inspiration.

Tailoring ad formats for different platforms

One size doesn't fit all in the world of social media ads. Here, we'll look at different ad formats for different platforms. We'll unlock the secrets of tailoring your captivating Canva designs to powerhouses such as Meta and Google Ads. By understanding each platform's unique layout and how users interact with content on each one, you'll learn to craft ads that speak directly to your audience, wherever they scroll.

How to do it...

While your captivating visuals will be a star player, maximizing their impact requires tailoring them to each platform's specific format requirements.

Here's a quick breakdown of the different platforms and the formats they provide:

- **Meta Ads (Facebook and Instagram)**:

Formats	Images	Carousels	Videos	Stories
Normal size	1,080x1,080 px	1,080x1,080 px (max 10 slides)	1,080x1,920 px	1,080x1,920 px
Resizing for Meta	Horizontal: 1,920x1,080 px Vertical: 1,080x1,920 px	Vertical: 1,080x1,920 px	1,080x1,080 px	1,080x1,080 px

Figure 7.2: Discovering Meta Ads formats

> **Note**
> Resizing your visual ads is essential for ensuring they are displayed optimally on different social media platforms, reaching a wider audience, and improving the overall performance of your campaigns. This is a great blog post that explains more: `https://soona.co/blog/why-image-resizing-matters`

- **Google Ads (Display Network and Search Network)**: This provides responsive display ads, image ads, and video ads:

  - **Responsive display ads**: These ads have no fixed size, instead using various combinations of width and height based on available space

  - **Image ads**: Recommended sizes vary depending on the ad network and location, but common sizes include the following:

    - **Leaderboard**: 728x90 pixels

    - **Medium rectangle**: 300x250 pixels

    - **Square**: 250x250 pixels

- **TikTok Ads**: These provide two main formats:

  - **In-feed video ads**: These are videos that are seamlessly integrated within user feeds. They provide greater control and targeting options for advertisers seeking precise results.

  - **Spark Ads**: These are organic TikTok videos used for promotion that offer a cost-effective way to amplify existing content.

  For both types of formats, the following holds true:

  - **Recommended aspect ratio**: 9:16 or 16:9

  - **Minimum resolution**: 640x360 pixels

  - **Maximum file size**: 200MB

  - **Video length**: 3 – 60 seconds (recommended length is under 30 seconds)

- **LinkedIn Ads**: These provide the following formats:

  - **Sponsored content**: This includes images, videos, or text displayed in user feeds.

  - **Text ads**: These consist of a small image, a headline, and a brief description. Think of them as the equivalent of classified ads in a newspaper, but for LinkedIn.

  - **Sponsored InMail**: These are ads sent as direct messages.

- **Image size**:

  - **Single image ads**: 1,200x627 pixels (aspect ratio 1.91:1)

  - **Carousel ads**: 1,080x1,080 pixels (square)

> **Note**
> These are general guidelines. Always check the latest specs from each platform for the most up-to-date information.

Once you know the format you want to use, you can now move over to Canva:

1. In Canva's dashboard, click on + **Create a design**:

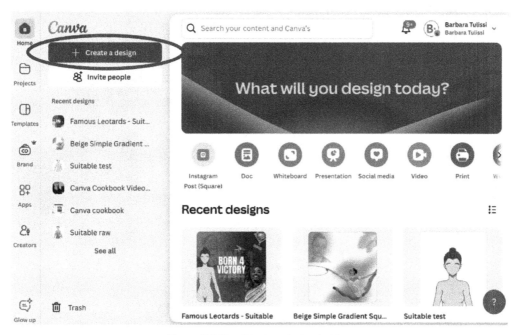

Figure 7.3: The Create a design button

2. The **Create a design** panel will appear. From the options on the left, choose **Custom size**. Now you can set your own size without choosing a pre-made Canva template. Let's suppose we want to create a generic square ad – in both the **Width** and **Height** fields, enter 1080.

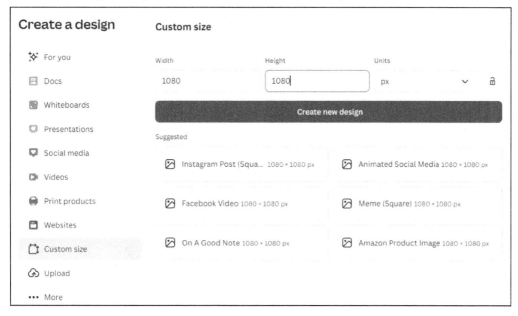

Figure 7.4: The Create a new design panel

3. Now imagine you have completed your design. As we said, you might need to resize your design for Meta's custom placements or for Google Ads. In our case, let's suppose we need to transform our Instagram post into an Instagram **story** instead.

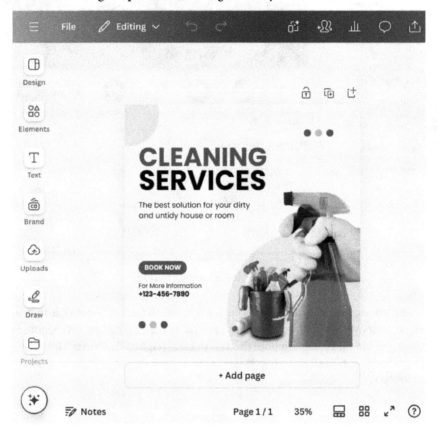

Figure 7.5: Our square ad

Resizing in Canva can be done in two different ways:

- If you are a free subscriber, I suggest you open a new project with its custom size, come back to the initial project, select all the elements within it, copy them, and paste them into the new project.

- If you are a paid Canva user, you can resize your design by using the **Resize** button on the top menu and setting the new measurements.

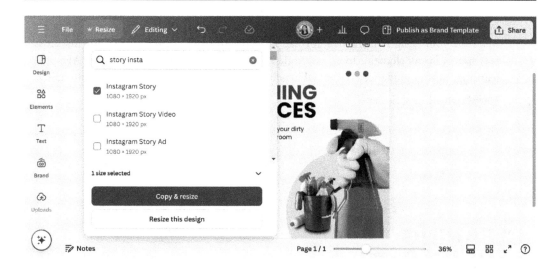

Figure 7.6: The Resize option

Then you can choose to copy and resize your project or simply resize it. Choose **Copy and resize** so you will have two projects: the square one and the vertical one (Instagram story).

Now here is our resized ad:

Figure 7.7: Our resized ad

While Canva's AI-powered Resize feature is helpful, you might need to make manual adjustments to ensure your design fits the new format perfectly. This could involve adjusting margins, text size, or layout elements to accommodate the vertical orientation. Remember, AI is still learning, so your guidance is essential in achieving the desired aesthetic and functionality.

Here is what I have done:

Figure 7.8: Our ad before and after the adjustments

Crafting stop-scrolling ads

Alright, alright, I confess! I've been holding back on the juicy ad-making secrets (muwahaha!). However, trust me, understanding the target audience and objective was crucial intel (if you haven't read those previous recipes, you should). Now, let's unleash your inner ad wizard!

In this recipe, I'll show you how to craft stop-scrolling showstoppers in Canva. We'll crack the code of captivating visuals, write headlines that hypnotize, and design ads so irresistible, that they'll have users hitting that **Learn More** button faster than you can say "cha-ching!".

In this recipe, I will guide you through the steps I undertook to create the following ad I used to promote my own web design academy (you can jump ahead to *Figure 7.18* to see what it looks like).

How to do it...

First up, we need to know the objective and target audience of the web design academy ad campaign:

- **Objective**: Sell my academy through a monthly membership.
- **Audience**: Italian freelancers, social media, and design students who want to improve their design skills are my target audience. According to my research, they are usually between 20-30 years old.

Now, to create the ad, follow these steps:

1. Open a 1,080x1,080 px project from your Canva dashboard.
2. Set a background that makes sense with the ad's topic. In this case, I created a custom background made of some screenshots and video thumbnails. To replicate mine, follow these steps:

    I. Browse **Elements** for the square frame element. Add it to your design, rotate it, and duplicate it several times to create asymmetrical diagonals.

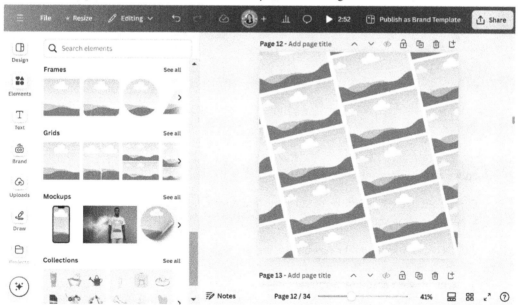

Figure 7.9: Creating our background

II.   Fill the frames with some screenshots related to an online academy to give a sort of preview of what the user will find inside once they purchase the membership or the course (of course, you probably don't have screenshots of my courses but you get the idea!).

III.   I also prefer to add a gradient overlay to maintain visual consistency with my brand's palette.

Here is the result so far:

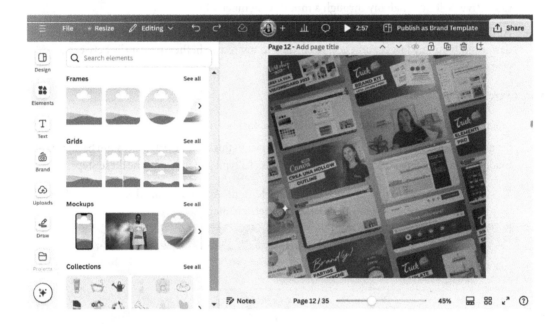

Figure 7.10: Finishing our background

3. Then we want to divide the ad into two parts:

    • On the left, we will add text, because my audience read from left to right, so I wanted to keep the reading smooth:

        i.   To do so, you can add a text box (using the *T* shortcut) to write your headline to make the user better understand what the ad's topic is. Then add another text box and fill it with all your academy features.

        ii.   Since the text is not readable this way, we need to add an underlay beneath it. We can search for a wavy element to give a sense of dynamicity to our ad.

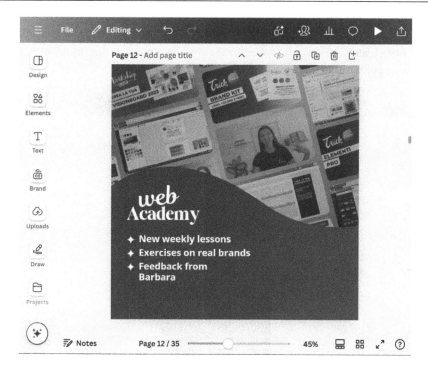

Figure 7.11: Adding the text

- On the right, we will add images of phones with their screens, showing screenshots of my academy. This will help the user understand that they can also follow the lessons from their smartphone and give the idea of a tangible service:

Figure 7.12: Finding a spot for our mockup

To create these mockups, follow these steps:

i.   I first created the image I wanted to show on the phone screen. In my case, I crafted a replica of the academy video interface:

Figure 7.13: Designing our mockup

ii.   Once ready, download the image.

iii.   Next, from the Canva dashboard, I browsed **Apps** and selected **Mockups**. In the search bar, I typed `smartphone` and looked for a dynamic smartphone mockup to give a sense of movement to my ad design.

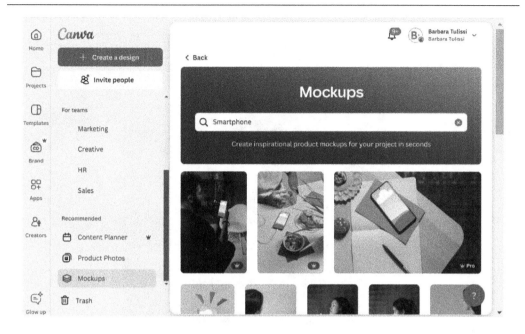

Figure 7.14: Searching in the Mockups tab

iv. Once I selected the mockup, Canva asked me to upload the image I had downloaded.
Once it is added to your mockup, it will be ready to be downloaded and uploaded to
your ad's project.

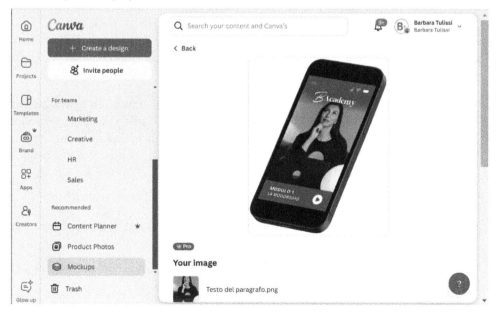

Figure 7.15: Finishing the mockup

Now here is the mockup in the ad (as you can see, I created a second mockup too):

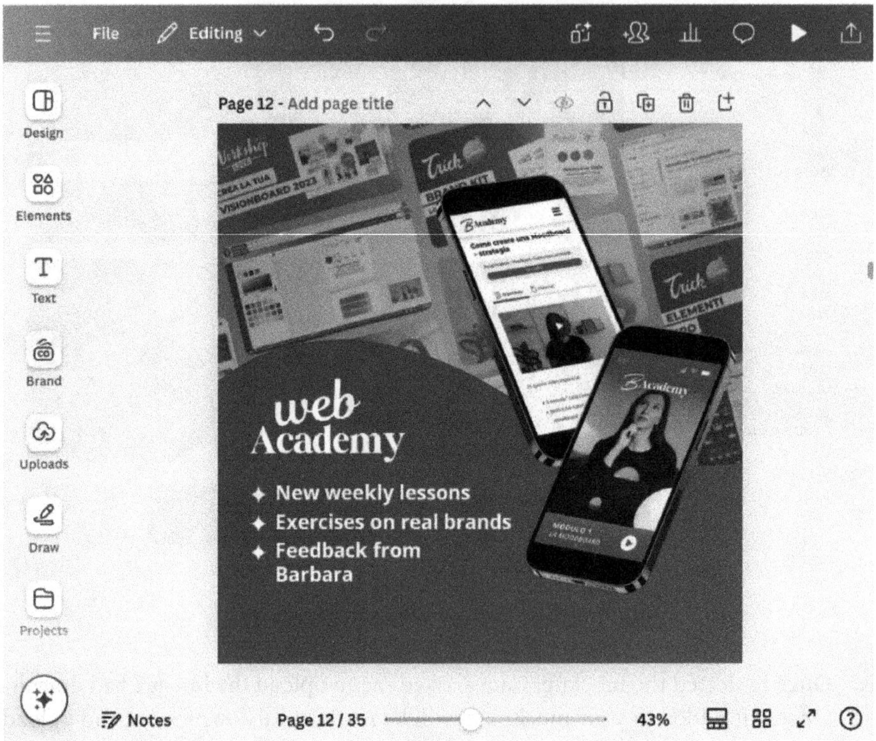

Figure 7.16: Adding the mockup to our ad

4. Finally, let's add the academy price. Begin by searching for the medal icon in the Elements search bar, and adding the shape to the design. Then you can add three text boxes for the price – this allows us to control the size of each part of the price:

    - In the first text box, add a dollar sign, then resize it so it appears small. This is because, from a neuromarketing perspective, the size of the dollar symbol can subtly influence perception. A smaller dollar symbol can create a psychological sense of affordability, making the price appear less daunting. Conversely, a large dollar symbol might emphasize the cost and potentially deter customers.

    - In the second and third text boxes, you can add the dollars and cents, respectively:

      - Following a similar logic to the dollar sign, making the cents text smaller also makes the price feel smaller.

      - Plus, choosing a price such as $9.99 instead of $10 makes the first option sound significantly cheaper (when it's really not).

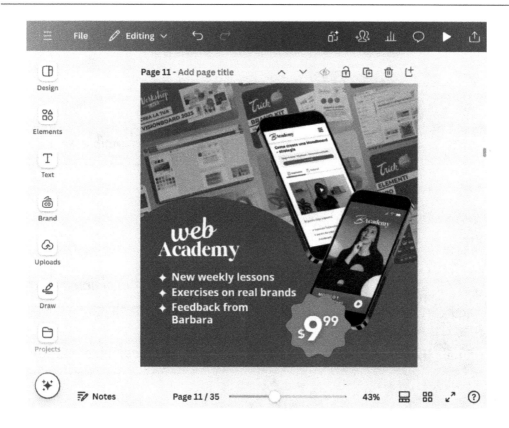

Figure 7.17: Completing our ad

> **Note**
>
> As you might see, I did not craft a CTA button, but that's because Meta also provides a button right below the ad itself once the campaign has been launched. However, if you're wondering how to create an effective button, you can jump to the last recipe of this chapter!

Now that we've created our ad, let's take a step back and evaluate our design. We've effectively transformed an intangible service into a tangible concept using a visually appealing mockup.

In addition to the visuals, we've included explanatory text to provide context and help users understand the value of our service. By clearly displaying cost information, we demonstrate transparency and build trust with potential customers.

Remember, market testing is essential for refining your ad and ensuring it resonates with your target audience.

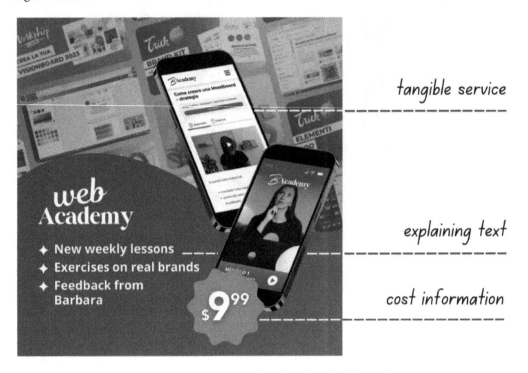

Figure 7.18: Anatomy of a well-performing Meta ad

There's more...

We've looked at how I created the ad campaign for my web academy courses. However, why not look at another example?

Nicola, the CMO of a local roof company with a reputation for quality and fair pricing, was facing a lead generation headache. Their Meta ads, while bringing in leads, were not bringing in actual customers. The company secretary, Sara, spent hours calling leads only to discover they were completely unaware of the company's free estimate policy or its competitive pricing. That's when I came in to help.

Taking a closer look at Nicola's existing ads, it was clear the problem wasn't the message itself, but the way it was delivered. Stock photos of generic roofs felt impersonal, and text-heavy content overloaded viewers with technical jargon. These ads lacked the emotional connection needed to grab attention and nurture leads.

Figure 7.19: Before and after the ad makeover

To craft a more compelling narrative, we decided to focus on visual storytelling. We swapped the generic photos for a high-quality image showcasing a recent project, highlighting the company's service features.

However, reaching the right audience was just as important. Meta's powerful targeting options allowed us to pinpoint homeowners in specific demographics most likely to need roof repairs. We further enhanced this by utilizing an image of a familiar local landmark to geographically connect with potential clients.

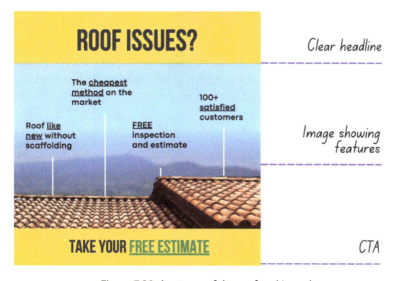

Figure 7.20: Anatomy of the roof-making ad

The results were like patching a leaky roof – transformative. The cost per lead dropped significantly, exceeding Nicola's target of €15. More importantly, the leads themselves were far more qualified. Homeowners were now aware of the company's free estimates and competitive pricing, leading to a much higher conversion rate from leads to booked consultations.

This company's story is a testament to the power of strategic ad design. By crafting visuals that resonate with the audience, delivering a clear and valuable message, and targeting the right demographic, Meta ads can be transformed from leaky lead generators into powerful tools for business growth.

There's even more...

Canva is a powerful tool for creating stunning visuals, but crafting effective ads for Meta (Facebook and Instagram) and Google requires a strategic approach. Let's dive into the dos and don'ts to help you conquer the world of online advertising:

Dos	Don'ts
Simplicity is key: A clear and concise message is crucial. Avoid clutter – use high-quality visuals, strong fonts, and minimal text to make your message impactful at a glance.	**AI images**: For now, it seems that they are unpopular for advertising on social media.
Embrace communicative images: People connect with emotions. Use visuals and messaging that evoke a positive feeling relevant to your product or service. Also, facial expressions can help the perception of your product since people easily empathize with human faces.	**Poorly illuminated images of human faces and shapes**: Even if your brand embraces the dark mood, remember that Meta, like Google Ads, loves bright faces and high-quality images while despising grainy and blurry pictures.
Psychological issues of color: Colors evoke emotions. In addition to the color palette, be careful to use colors such as yellow or red correctly. For example, if you want to sell a course, a bright red button on your CTA button may seem too intrusive and aggressive, while a blue button may give a sense of relaxation and won't make the viewer feel obligated to make a purchase.	**Grainy and blurry pictures**: Remember that using grainy or blurry visuals screams unprofessionalism. Use images that have a good resolution and are relevant to your brand.
Embrace whitespace: Don't cram everything into the frame. Whitespace creates breathing room, making your text and visuals pop.	**Stock photo clichés**: Overused stock photos can appear impersonal and generic. Look for unique, high-quality visuals that stand out from the crowd.

Dos	Don'ts
Use social proof: Social proof uses the "follow the crowd" mentality, where people are influenced by others' actions. In marketing, it builds trust by showcasing positive reviews, high engagement, or celebrity endorsements, ultimately driving conversions. Speaking about ads, using the Trustpilot badge or testimonials reviews can make the viewer trust your ad more.	**Text overload and poor font choice**: Nobody wants to read a novel in your ad. Keep the text concise and use bullet points or headlines to break up text blocks. Also, stick to clear, easy-to-read fonts. Avoid overly decorative or difficult-to-decipher styles.
Use scarcity and urgency: Using hourglass illustrations or countdowns can push viewers to act before missing the opportunity.	**Neglect mobile optimization**: Most ad viewing happens on mobile devices. Ensure your ads are clear and easy to read on smaller screens.
One clear CTA: Craft a focused CTA for each ad. Avoid overwhelming your audience with multiple requests. A single, clear CTA will guide users toward the desired outcome, maximizing your campaign's effectiveness.	**Overdo it with CTAs**: Don't include too many CTAs, as this can confuse the reader. Just provide them with one clear CTA instead.
Pay attention to details: Crafting effective ads requires careful attention to detail. While it might take an hour or more to create a visually appealing design, the time investment is worthwhile. By considering your ad's objectives and target audience, you can optimize your campaign for maximum impact and avoid wasted resources.	**Consider your paid ad as a white organic post**: Paid ads and organic posts serve different purposes. Paid ads focus on driving actions and require a more direct approach. Organic posts build relationships and community. Understanding these distinctions is crucial for effective content strategy.

Figure 7.21: Dos and don'ts when creating ads

While it's tempting to prioritize aesthetics, remember that understanding your target audience and aligning your ads with your business goals is crucial. Even the most visually appealing design might not resonate if it doesn't address the needs of your audience.

Don't be discouraged by any initial results. Continuously test different variations of your ads, including color changes and messaging tweaks. With persistence and data-driven insights, you'll refine your approach and achieve your marketing objectives.

Utilizing CTAs effectively

While creating clickable buttons in your Canva design might seem like the natural next step, it's not necessary for ads on platforms such as Meta or Google. Those platforms handle the overall click-ability of your ad for you.

The button you create in Canva serves a different purpose. It's a visual cue, a way to tell viewers, "Hey, there's something you can do here!" It's like a mini billboard within your ad, enticing clicks and directing attention toward the action you want them to take.

When we use a button with some text over it in ads, we call it a CTA.

CTAs allow you to transform your viewers from passive observers into engaged participants. In this recipe, I'll walk you through how to create them directly within Canva, and even provide you with a couple of bonus tips to enhance them.

How to do it...

To create a CTA, follow these steps:

1. First, we need a button. There are two ways to create a button in Canva:

    *   Head over to the **Elements** panel on the left-hand side of your Canva workspace. Search for `buttons` and choose your favorite one. Some elements allow you to change their color and dimensions, but others just don't.

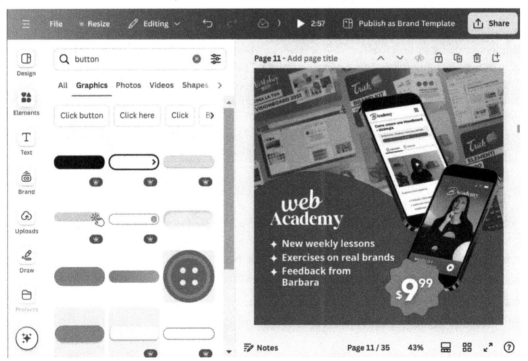

Figure 7.22: Finding buttons in the Elements panel

- Or, within the **Elements** panel, scroll down to the **Shapes** section and choose a rectangle (or use the *R* shortcut to directly create a rectangle). This way, you can create your own button, making its corners round and changing its dimensions.

2. Regardless of which method you choose, drag the button you want into your project.

3. Customize the button's design by double-clicking the button to access its editing options. Here's your chance to make it visually pop! Play with different colors – consider your brand palette or use a contrasting color to make it stand out. You can also adjust the button's size and position to best suit your design.

4. Then, craft the text inside the CTA button:

    - If you chose a button element from the **Elements** panel, you can add a text box using the *T* shortcut, placing it over your button and adding the text.

    - If you created your custom button with a shape, then you can just click inside the shape to add your text.

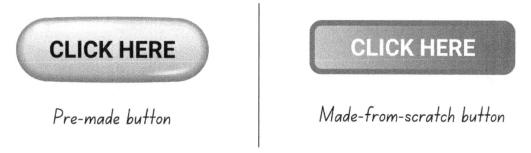

Figure 7.23: A pre-made button and a made-from-scratch button

There's more...

Here are a couple of bonus tips when creating a CTA:

- **A psychological note on CTA placement**: While crafting your button, keep strategic placement in mind. A CTA placed at the very beginning of your design, before viewers have a chance to understand your message, can come across as pushy. For optimal impact, consider placing your CTA toward the end of the design, allowing viewers time to read and evaluate your offer.

- **Highlighting your CTA**: If you want to make sure your CTA truly shines, consider adding a subtle pointer or even a picture of a person pointing and looking directly at the CTA. This playful nudge can subconsciously draw viewers' attention and encourage them to click.

Figure 7.24: Using a person to highlight a CTA

8

Developing Effective Marketing Documents

Developing marketing documents is a crucial new skill in today's marketing landscape. Whether you're a small business owner, a freelancer, or part of a marketing team, the ability to create clear and compelling marketing materials is a game-changer. It empowers you to effectively communicate your brand story, convert leads into customers, and ultimately achieve your marketing goals.

In this chapter, we'll delve into the world of crafting impactful marketing materials using Canva. We'll be dissecting the key elements that make a marketing document sing, from conceptualizing clear messaging to choosing the right visuals. By the end of this journey, you'll have a toolkit filled with practical strategies to design marketing documents that not only grab attention but also resonate with your target audience.

So, buckle up and get ready to unleash your inner marketing document maestro!

In this chapter, you will cover the following recipes:

- Creating a digital business card
- Transforming an event flyer
- Creating a template for invoices and quotes
- Creating an email signature

Creating a digital business card

Forget the paper business cards that end up in the recycling bin! In this recipe, I'll show you how to craft a digital business card in Canva. This eco-friendly alternative lets you ditch the outdated paper approach, especially for Millennials and Gen Z who connect on LinkedIn or tap phones with **near-field communication (NFC)**.

> **Note**
>
> If you have doubts about what NFC means, let me refresh! **NFC** is a technology that allows devices such as smartphones to exchange data when they're very close to each other. It's used for contactless payments, sharing files, and connecting to other devices.

So, let's design a digital business card so innovative that they'll want to keep it on hand (or rather, in their phone).

How to do it...

Imagine a business card that goes beyond traditional limits. Include all essential information such as your name, job title, and contact details, and then leverage a QR code to unlock a world of additional content. This digital extension can link to your portfolio, social media, or even a personalized landing page.

Here's how to do it:

1. Open Canva and start a new project. Instead of using a horizontal format though, use a vertical layout with dimensions of 55x80 mm. This simple twist will make your card stand out from the crowd!

    The business card will have two "pages" – the first page will provide your business details and the second page will provide the QR code to your business's website.

2. To start developing the first page, do the following:

    I. Use text boxes (with the *T* shortcut) to add all of your essential details:

        *   **Your name**: Make sure it is big and readable.

        *   **Your job title**: Briefly explain what you do (for example, "Content Creator" or "Web Development Ninja").

        *   **Your contact details**: Include your phone number, email, and website (if applicable).

        *   **The "hilarious" location (optional)**: Feeling playful? Add a fun location description (think "Internet Oasis").

    II. Add an image of you or something that represents your business – in my case, I uploaded my Instagram profile picture and dragged and dropped it into my design.

III.   Unleash your creativity, but prioritize clarity. The market's trend is minimalism so avoid overcluttering your design. In my case, I added some line shapes in two different colors, creating a simple alternating pattern.

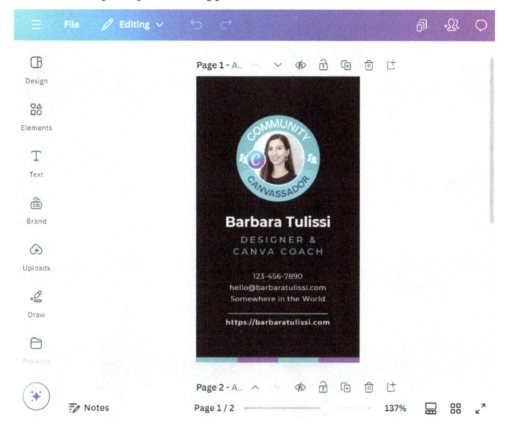

Figure 8.1: Customization of the front of our business card

3.   Now, let's create the second page for the QR code. Duplicate the page and remove the elements you do not need – I decided to keep the line pattern at the bottom of the page to keep a sense of consistency.

4.   To add the QR code, click **Apps** in the left toolbar, search QR, and select **QR code**.

> **Note**
>
> As you can see in *Figure 8.2*, there are lots of different integrated apps in Canva that can help you create impactful QR codes. However, these apps offer more creative QR code features, which can create complexity for you, as the designer, and those scanning the card. Instead, I prefer to keep things simple and use the classic **QR code** app.

5.   From the **QR code** menu, you can copy the URL or your LinkedIn, Instagram, or website into the **URL** box:

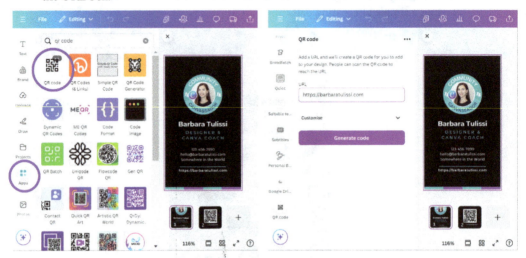

Figure 8.2: The QR code app

6.   Now, place the QR code on the second page. Once added, underneath, add a new text box that includes the destination URL. This gives the viewer extra understanding (and reassurance) of where the QR code will take them.

Here is the result of my digital business card:

Figure 8.3: My business card, with a QR code

7. Once you're happy with your design, you can export it as a `.png` or `.pdf` file and save it into your gallery or phone files. Then, during business meetings and events, you can send the digital card to potential clients directly or you can let them scan the QR code.

There's more...

As we said, people can forget that they have received your business card quickly, and then your brand already has faded from memory. But what if your card could be different? What if it was so cool, useful, or fun that someone would want to keep it?

Here's the key: it needs to be something people want to hold onto, whether it's because it's beautiful, funny, or surprisingly useful. The best part? This totally depends on your niche! Here are some inspiring examples:

- **Architectural artistry**: An architect's business card with a tiny ruler cleverly incorporated at the top – practical and oh-so-handy!

- **Picture perfect**: A photographer's business card is a mini print showcasing their stunning work.

- **Brews and business**: A brewery that uses coasters as their business cards – genius for grabbing attention and doubling as a useful drink holder.

Figure 8.4: Unique business cards

Also, choosing the right paper or material can not only enhance how information is displayed on your card but also make it stand out from the crowd. Choosing an irregular shape such as a half moon, a heart, or a round shape can link to your brand and make it stand out.

Figure 8.5: More unique business cards

Let's add a dash of fun to those business cards! While it might be tough to incorporate all five senses (imagine a business card that smells like pizza), some clever folks are already pushing the boundaries.

For example, beauty salons might use a touch of perfume on their cards, leaving a lingering scent that reminds you of their services. DJs could include a QR code that links to their hottest Spotify playlists, letting you get a taste of their musical style. Now, edible business cards? That might be a bit tricky (although a tiny cookie card from a bakery sounds pretty tempting).

Transforming an event flyer

Flyers are often underestimated as marketing tools, but they hold immense power when designed and distributed strategically. This recipe will guide you through a design makeover, transforming a dull and ineffective flyer into a design that grabs attention and gets results. Ready, steady... go!

Getting ready

Imagine this: a local client approaches you, needing a captivating flyer to promote their summer camp. They hand you the current design, eager to draw in more campers. Intrigued, you take a close look:

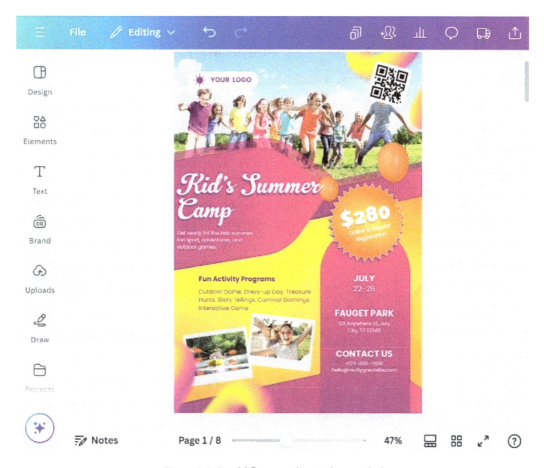

Figure 8.6: An old flyer needing to be restyled

> **Note**
> You can find this flyer template here so you can follow along with the makeover exercise: `https://partner.canva.com/XYb4jo`.

Before diving into specific fixes, I challenge you to train your designer's eye. Can you spot any areas for improvement on your own? Take a moment to analyze the design – what elements seem to work, and what could be better? Trust your instincts, then let's move on to reveal some potential areas for improvement together.

After reviewing the flyer, I have identified four main areas of improvement:

- **QR code**: We need a clear and user-friendly QR code. Avoid rotating it, as that might further confuse viewers. Moreover, placing the QR code over a child's face makes it look very clunky, don't you think?

- **Stock photo alert**: The image of the children playing seems like a generic stock image. While using stock images is okay, we want to choose one that feels authentic and realistic. Find one that evokes a genuine sense of childhood fun. You can take it yourself with your phone or even choose a library-stock picture, but look for one with natural lighting and avoid overly saturated images.

- **Legibility is key**: Text readability is paramount. We want to avoid placing text along the edges or using difficult-to-read fonts. Instead, we want to prioritize clarity and consistency.

- **Streamline the design**: This flyer feels cluttered and full of decorative elements that make the reader's attention fade away. Try to think like the flyer's reader: parents are looking for a fun and engaging summer environment for their children. One image showcasing happy kids playing together could be enough. Ditch the circled elements in the corners; they add visual noise.

Figure 8.7: The old flyer's weak points

Now that we've pinpointed the areas for improvement, let's dive into Canva and give this flyer a makeover!

> **Note**
>
> Sometimes, designers might not readily share source files or project links (we understand that design babies are precious). No worries; even if the original was an Illustrator project, Canva's magic lets you upload the final PDF file and edit it directly within Canva. To do so, from your Canva dashboard, click the **Create a design** button, where you can find the **Upload** option. Just drag and drop your desktop document or file to the Canva **Upload** tab and wait for it to be ready to be edited.

How to do it...

Let's tackle the improvements one by one:

1. First, let's fix the QR code. Move the QR code to a square position (0-degree rotation). We will keep it covering the child's face for now, and consider moving it shortly.

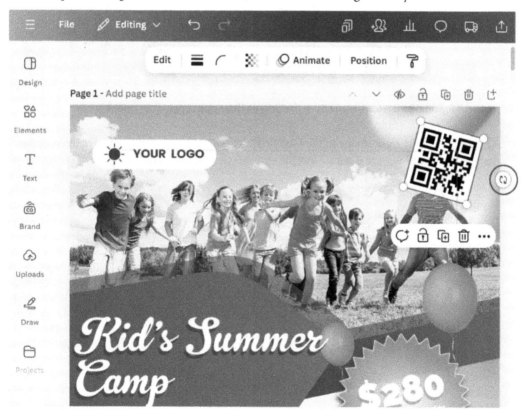

Figure 8.8: The Rotate tool

2. Next, let's replace the generic stock photo with a more authentic image. To streamline this process, you can connect your Google Drive with Canva if your photos reside there. Just click **Apps** in the left menu, search for `Google Drive`, open the app, and follow the guided steps to connect Google Drive to Canva. Now, all your Google Drive images and documents appear within the left-side panel of your Canva project, eliminating the need to download and upload them separately.

Figure 8.9: Adding a custom image from the Google Drive app (once it has been connected)

3. Once you find the right image in the Google Drive panel, drag and drop it over the original image. Canva will replace it automatically.

4. Now, let's think about improving readability:

I. The old flyer font was Gelato, however, Raleway creates a more readable experience by matching the flyer's existing sans-serif style. To change the font, then in the popup menu, click the current font name. You will then be presented with a list where you can pick the new font style.

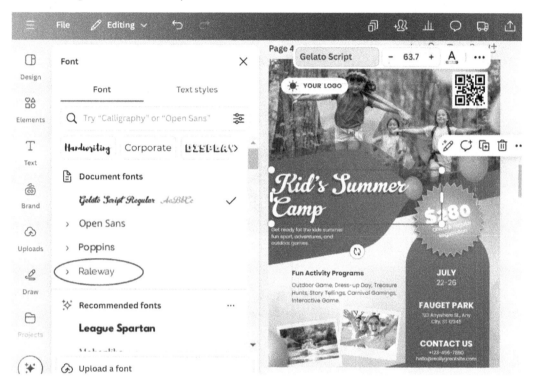

Figure 8.10: Changing the current font to Raleway

II.   Previously, the text was too close to the edge of the flyer. To help, go to **File | Settings | Show Margins**). This allows you to see the margins and move the text away from the flyer's edges.

III.   At this point, we can also reduce the font size, format it better with bold, and add shading. To create the shade, select the text box and within the toolbar, look for **Effects**. Then, in the new side panel, choose **Shadow**. Now, you can adjust the offset, direction, blur, transparency, and color of your text's shadow.

Figure 8.11: Fixing typography and applying effects

IV.   Next, I adjusted the summer camp price text by selecting a darker shade from the flyer's color palette. The previous light color against the yellow background was causing difficulty in reading the price. The darker shade creates a stronger contrast, making the text pop and easier to see.

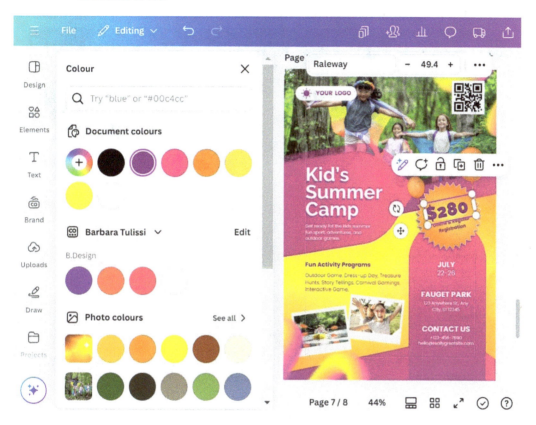

Figure 8.12: Making the font contrast with the background stronger

V.   If you have Canva Pro, you can effortlessly switch fonts and colors according to your brand kit. Simply click **Project** on the left-hand panel, then **Style**. Once you've selected your brand kit, just click as many times as you need on your color palette and your fonts box. Canva will randomly change colors and fonts to all the elements in your design. Play around until you find the perfect match!

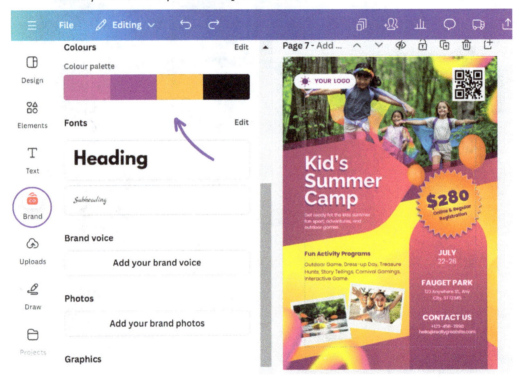

Figure 8.13: Using the Brand palette

5.   Finally, let's look at streamlining the design:

I.   Now that the new top image conveys the childhood excitement of camp in a more authentic way, we don't need the extra Polaroid images, so remove them.

II. Let's also relocate the QR code to the area previously occupied by the polaroids, simply moving it closer to the contact information (since QR codes often link to websites or contact details).

Now, let's see what our flyer looks like:

Figure 8.14: Before and after the flyer makeover

Creating a template for invoices and quotes

Invoices are more than just receipts; they're marketing tools that reflect your brand's professionalism and leave a lasting impression on clients. A well-designed invoice can enhance your brand identity, streamline your billing process, and improve client satisfaction.

Let's elevate your billing process with Canva. In this recipe, we'll guide you through creating customized invoices that not only look professional but also streamline your workflow.

How to do it...

Let's dive into the world of Invoices. Ready? Let's go!

1. Open Canva and create a new project. You can either search for `Freelance Invoice` to find an appropriate template or you can start a blank document, choosing a document size that works well for you (i.e., A4 or Letter).

2. A good place to start is by adding your brand's logo. Click **Uploads** on the left-hand panel and upload your logo (or a relevant image representing your digital marketing services). Drag and drop the logo onto your document. Position it prominently at the top of the invoice.

3. Then, let's add two text boxes using the *T* shortcut:

    - The first should be placed under the logo, containing your client's information

    - The second should be placed to the right, containing the invoice number and issue date

4. Let's design and fill our table: on the left-hand side of Canva, select **Elements** and find the **Tables** section. From here, Canva offers a variety of pre-designed table layouts with different styles and numbers of rows and columns. Browse the options and select one that suits your needs. Click the chosen table layout, then drag it onto your design workspace to place it where you want it.

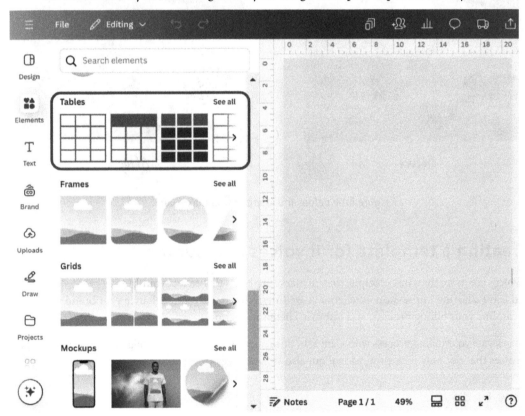

Figure 8.15: Using the Tables feature

5. Double-click on the table to edit the text within each cell. Rename the columns to `Item`, `Quantity`, `Unit Price`, and `Total`. Modify the font style, size, and color of the table text to match your brand and the design.

6. Adjust the number of rows as needed, based on the number of services offered in the invoice.

7. Below the table, add text boxes (*T*) for the following:

   - **Subtotal**: You have to manually calculate the sum of all "amounts" entries in the table before writing it down in the text box.

   - **Tax (if applicable)**: Enter the tax percentage and calculate the total tax amount.

   - **Total**: To calculate the total, add the amount of tax to the subtotal cost of the items. Enter this combined value into the total text box.

8. To actually get paid, make sure to share your bank account details using a text box. I also like to add *Thank you* to delight my clients, choosing a script-like font to make it look handwritten.

   Here is my final result:

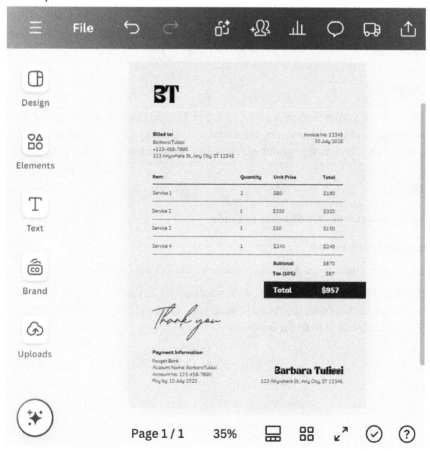

Figure 8.16: My invoice result

9. Once satisfied with your design, click **Download** and choose **PDF Print** for a printable version or **PDF Standard** for a digital copy. Canva also allows you to share the invoice as a link directly from the platform by clicking **Share**.

> **Bonus Tip**
>
> Save your completed invoice design as a template in Canva. This allows you to easily duplicate it for future projects and update the client and invoice details for each new client. Consider adding a brief bio or portfolio link at the bottom of your invoice to showcase your work and build brand recognition.

Creating an email signature

In today's digital age, a well-crafted email signature can leave a lasting impression and enhance your professional brand. In this recipe, we'll explore how to create clickable signatures using Canva and Google Docs, empowering you to add interactive elements to your emails.

Getting ready...

For this recipe, you will need a Google account to access Google Docs. I will then show you how to add the email signature in Gmail, however, you could do this using a different email provider. If you don't succeed using another email provider, please see the note box at the end of the recipe.

How to do it...

Let's create an email signature. We will start in Canva:

1. Open a 100x100 px project.
2. On the left side menu, open **Apps**, then search and select **Brandfetch**.
3. Search for Instagram, Facebook, TikTok, or whatever social media you want to be followed by your email reader. Let's take the case of Instagram – drag and drop the Instagram logo within your project and scale it to fit the borders.

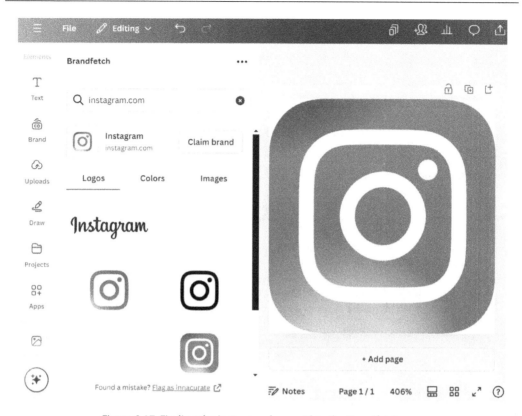

Figure 8.17: Finding the Instagram logo within the Brandfetch app

4. Add a new page and search for another social media logo you will need for your email signature. Drag the icon into the page and scale it to fit the borders.

5. Repeat this process, creating a page per logo.

6. Download all the brand icons you need as .png files with transparent backgrounds. If you have Canva Pro, you can use the **Background Removal** option, or if you are using the free version, you can use remove.bg.

Note

We used the use the **Background Removal** option and remove.bg back in *Chapter 3*, in the *Improving your profile image* recipe.

Now, let's make our signature clickable in Google Docs:

1. Open your Google account and navigate to the **Docs** option.

2. Open a new Google document, click **Insert**, and select **Table**.

3. Create a table with one row and two columns:

   - Within the first column, insert your brand logo (using **Insert| Picture**) and resize it to fit the column borders

   - In the second row, do the following:

     - Write your full name and job title; I suggest you use some style, such as bolding your full name, to emphasize it, and styling your job title in italics, to differentiate it

     - Underneath, add the social media icons you downloaded from Canva (using **Insert| Picture** again) and position them in a row

4. Now, click on the first social media logo and select the link icon from the toolbar. Then, paste the link to your social media account in the pop-up box and click **Apply**.

Figure 8.18: Finding the link option within Google Docs

Repeat this step for the other social media logos you added.

5. Now, let's clean up the design a little bit. Click on one of the table borders, hold *Ctrl* (Windows) or *Shift* (Mac), and select the others. Once every border has been selected, click on the border icon and set the border thickness to **0 pt** – this way, you will hide the borders.

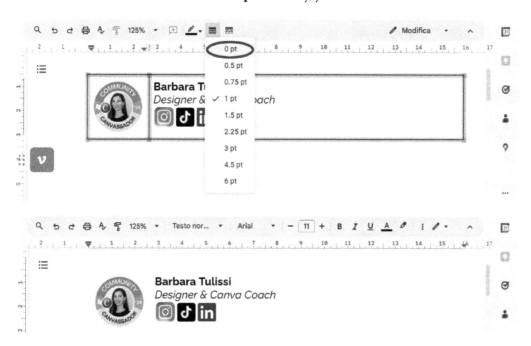

Figure 8.19: Hiding the table borders

6. Now, select your whole Google Doc design by pressing *Ctrl + A* (Windows) or *Cmd + A* (Mac), copy the selected elements using *Ctrl+C* (Windows) or *Cmd+C* (Mac) and open your Gmail account.

In Gmail, do the following:

1. Go to your Gmail **Settings** and select **See all settings**.

2. Scroll down to the **General** tab, click **Signature**, and then click + **Create new**.

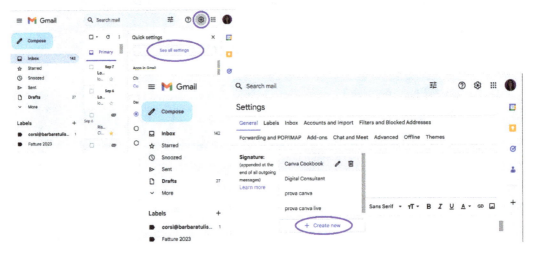

Figure 8.20: Finding the Signature option in Gmail

3. In the **Signature** field, paste your design from Google Docs using *Ctrl+V* (Windows) or *Cmd+V* (Mac).

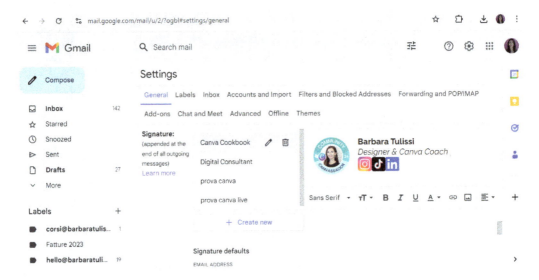

Figure 8.21: Copying and pasting your signature in Gmail

4.   Click **Save changes**.

Now, you are ready to send super professional emails that really engage the reader:

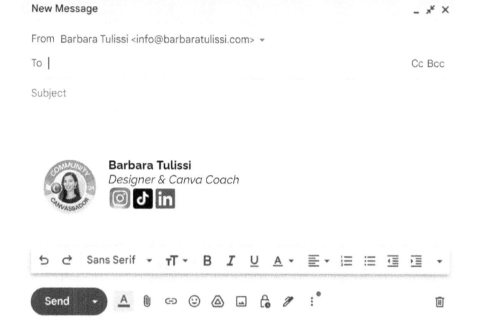

Figure 8.22: Your email signature in an email

> Note
>
> If you don't succeed in adding your signature using another email provider, you can download your whole signature as an image (.jpg or .png) and upload the image at the end of your email.

9

Ensuring Accessibility and Inclusivity in Your Designs

Have you ever encountered a website or document that was so frustrating to navigate that you wanted to throw your device out the window? Microscopic fonts, jarring color contrasts, and confusing layouts are all too common in today's digital world.

Inclusive design benefits everyone, not just helping those who have disabilities. Imagine struggling to read your phone on a sunny beach or experiencing eye strain after a long day in front of a screen. Accessible design principles make digital content usable for all, regardless of their temporary or permanent circumstances.

By following guidelines such as the **Web Content Accessibility Guidelines (WCAG)**, we can create designs that are not only visually appealing but also functional and inclusive. The WCAG, developed by the W3C, provide a global standard for making web content accessible to people with disabilities. By understanding and implementing the WCAG principles, we can ensure that our designs are perceivable, operable, understandable, and robust for everyone.

This chapter will equip you with the knowledge and tools to create designs that break down barriers and provide a positive user experience for all. Let's dive in and discover how to create designs that truly make a difference.

In this chapter, we will have a quick look at the WCAG before covering the following recipes:

- Reviewing the WCAG
- Creating readable text and typography
- Using alt text for images and graphics
- Enabling captions on videos and audio
- Creating images using AI

Reviewing the WCAG

The WCAG is a set of guidelines developed by the **World Wide Web Consortium (W3C)** to ensure that web content is accessible to people with disabilities. The guidelines are based on four principles:

- *Perceivable*: Information and user interface components must be presented to users in ways they can perceive

- *Operable*: User interface components and navigation must be operable

- *Understandable*: Information and user interface components must be understandable

- *Robust*: Content must be robust enough to be interpreted by a variety of user agents, including assistive technologies

Further, based on these principles, the guidelines are divided into three levels of conformance:

- *Level A*: These are the most basic requirements for accessibility

- *Level AA*: These are more stringent requirements than Level A

- *Level AAA*: These are the most stringent requirements, more than Levels A and AA

The WCAG is constantly being updated to reflect new technologies and best practices. The latest version of the guidelines is WCAG 2.2, which was published in October 2023.

Here are some of the specific requirements of the WCAG guidelines:

- *Text alternatives*: All non-text content, such as images and videos, must have text alternatives that provide the same information

- *Color contrast*: There must be sufficient contrast between foreground and background colors to make text and images readable

- *Keyboard accessibility*: All functionality must be accessible using a keyboard

- *Focus management*: Users must be able to easily navigate between user interface components using the keyboard

- *Time-based media*: Time-based media, such as videos and audio, must have captions or transcripts

- *Adaptable*: Content must be adaptable to different user agents and display sizes

The WCAG is a valuable resource for web developers and content creators who want to ensure that their websites and applications are accessible to everyone. You can find more details here: `https://www.w3.org/TR/WCAG20/`. By following the guidelines, you can help to make the web a more inclusive place for people with disabilities.

Creating readable text and typography

Crafting beautiful designs is great, but ensuring that everyone can access and understand your message is even better. This recipe focuses on creating readable text and typography in Canva, specifically with accessibility and inclusivity in mind.

We'll quickly look at some best practices for choosing clear fonts, appropriate sizing, and effective color contrast to make your designs user-friendly, then jump into the Design Accessibility Checker, an essential tool to ensure accessibility in Canva.

> **Note**
>
> Unfortunately, the Design Accessibility Checker's availability may vary depending on your Canva account type and region.

Getting ready

Before we dive into accessibility and inclusivity tips, let's look at some general graphic design best practices when it comes to using text in your projects:

- *Opt for sans-serif fonts*: Sans-serif fonts lack the decorative flourishes found in typical serif fonts, making them easier to read on screens and at smaller sizes. Popular choices include Arial, Helvetica, and Open Sans.

- *Consider serif fonts for print*: While sans-serif fonts are excellent for digital, serif fonts (such as Times New Roman and Garamond) are traditionally preferred for print. Their serifs (small strokes at the ends of letters) can improve readability on paper, especially for longer blocks of text.

- *Avoid script fonts*: While stylish, script fonts can be difficult to decipher, especially for people with visual impairments. Save them for decorative purposes only.

- *Limit font variety*: Using too many different fonts can create visual clutter and hinder readability. Stick to two or three fonts for a cohesive look.

- *Headline hierarchy*: Use larger fonts for headings and titles to establish hierarchy and guide readers. A good rule of thumb is 16pt or higher for main titles, and 12–14pt for subheadings.

- *Mobile-first approach*: Consider how your design will look on smaller screens. Ensure text remains legible when viewed on smartphones.

- *Dark text on light background (or vice versa)*: This is the safest approach for optimal readability. Tools such as Canva Color Wheel (`https://www.canva.com/colors/color-wheel/`) can help you find complementary color combinations.

- *Be aware of color blindness*: Consider how your design translates for people with color blindness. Tools such as Coblis Color Simulator (`https://www.color-blindness.com/coblis-color-blindness-simulator/`) can help you preview your design for different types of color blindness.

How to do it...

Now, let's turn to Canva's built-in Design Accessibility Checker, which helps you identify some of these potential issues:

1. Before running the Design Accessibility Checker, ensure your text and background elements are finalized. This allows the tool to accurately assess the contrast ratio.

2. Now, go to **File** | **Accessibility** and click the **Check design accessibility** button:

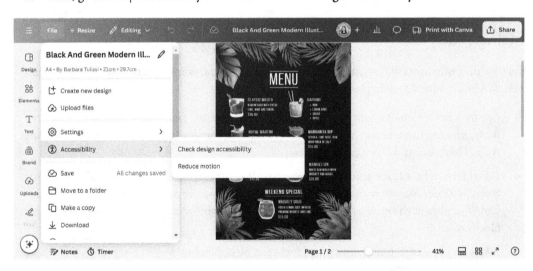

Figure 9.1: Finding the Design Accessibility Checker in Canva

3. A **Design Accessibility** panel will appear on the right. Here, Canva will analyze your design and display any accessibility issues, with issues marked as blue circles:

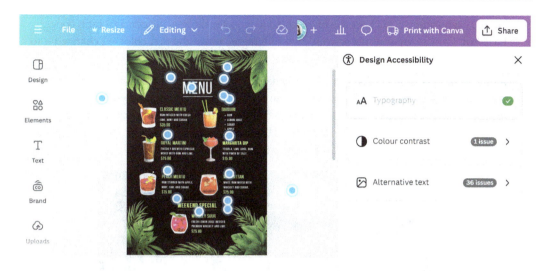

Figure 9.2: The Design Accessibility panel

As you can see in *Figure 9.2*, the **Design Accessibility** panel has identified issues with alternative text and color contrast. We will take a look at the first problem in the *Using alt text for images and graphics* recipe later in the chapter, so here we will focus on color contrast.

When you click the issue, you will see a suggestion for improvement, such as a different text color or background adjustment.

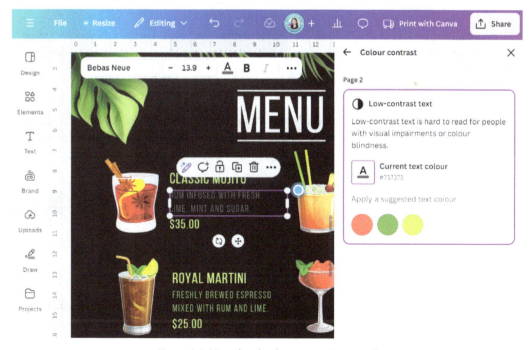

Figure 9.3: How the checker suggestions work

4. To make adjustments, click on the highlighted area to see the specific contrast ratio concern. Based on Canva's suggestions or your own judgment, adjust the text color – I changed it to white, a background color, or both to create a higher contrast ratio.

5. In my experience, I noted that Canva hardly detects issues with typography, which we can see is the case back in *Figure 9.2*. However, we can check it manually on our own. When it comes to typography, we'll focus on text hierarchy. Giving hierarchy to your information means giving a different emphasis to titles (H1), subtitles (H2, H3, etc.), and paragraphs. In *Figure 9.4*, you can also see how we changed the font color to further emphasize the hierarchy.

Figure 9.4: Heading hierarchy

By organizing content in a logical and predictable manner, you make it easier for users, including those with disabilities, to navigate and understand your design.

6. To further improve hierarchy within your paragraphs, you can use bullet points or numbered lists for readers to easily scan information, and find the relevant information for them.

Get help from the Canva Pro feature Magic Write, which will help you rework texts using integrated AI. To activate Magic Write, double-click on the textbox and the **Magic Write** option will appear. Here, you can write your prompt, such as `Turn it into a list`.

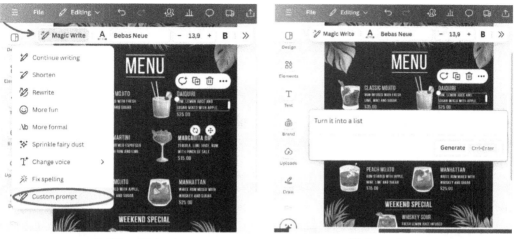

Find Magic Write   *Write a custom promt*

Figure 9.5: Using AI to help with hierarchy

Once you have entered the prompt, Magic Write will provide a suggestion on what content to add. If you're happy with it, just click **Replace**, and the content will be updated in your project.

Replace the outcome   *Final result*

Figure 9.6: Using AI to turn text into a list

7.   Finally, in Canva, you can utilize spell check and grammar tools to ensure your text is error-free and professional. Like other word processors, these tools are automatic and work as you type – any potential errors will be highlighted with a red underline. Right-click on the underlined word to see suggested corrections.

> **Note**
> Even if your Canva account doesn't have the built-in Accessibility Checker yet, following general best practices for color contrast and clear typography will significantly improve the accessibility of your designs.

There's more...

Does your brand speak to everyone? In today's diverse world, as well as the content being readable, inclusive communication is also key. Let's look at some ways to do this:

- *Avoid gendered imagery*: We all know the limitations of stereotypes. Does a CEO have to be a white man in a suit? Absolutely not! Canva's **Elements** library is vast, but the search terms that creators use might not always reflect your vision of inclusivity. Here's a secret tip: instead of typing CEO in the search bar, close your eyes and imagine what a CEO might look like for your target audience. Then, translate that vision into keywords! For example, instead of CEO, try searching with terms such as `confident woman leading team` or `young entrepreneur casual attire`. Strive to move beyond stereotypical portrayals in your designs. Don't always show women as caregivers or men as leaders.

- *Showcase real people*: Feature a variety of ethnicities, ages, genders, body types, and abilities in your designs. You might not know but older consumers are a powerful and growing demographic; however, according to a survey by AARP, an organization representing older adults in the United States, many older consumers feel overlooked, stereotyped, and not accurately portrayed in advertising (`https://advertise.aarp.org/50-insights/aarp-makes-case-for-older-audiences`). Including people older than 50 in your campaigns helps your marketing reflect reality and gives you a better chance of tapping into this growing market. Utilize Canva's extensive stock photo library such as Pexels, Unsplash, and Pixabay, which you can find in Canva's **App** section. Search filters allow you to find images based on ethnicity, age, gender, and more. Refine your search further using keywords such as `diverse team` or `multiracial group`.

- *Be considerate when talking about disabilities*: When talking about disabilities, consider whether person-first language or identity-first language is the most respectful to the particular community you are talking about. If you are creating content about disabilities for a client, you can talk to them about the target audience and the best language to use.

Using alt text for images and graphics

Images and graphics are powerful tools in your Canva designs, but what if some viewers can't see them? Alt text, or alternative text, acts like a narrator for your visuals, describing them to people who can't see them. This could be due to visual impairments, using screen readers, or even just slow internet connections where images take time to load.

This recipe tackles adding alt text, ensuring everyone understands your visuals. By including alt text, you'll create more inclusive designs that reach a wider audience.

How to do it...

To add alt text to an image, follow these instructions:

1. With a project open, click on the image or graphic you want to add alt text to.

2. Depending on your Canva version, you may see three dots (**...**) or a gear icon. Click the one you see, then from the menu, select **Alternative text** (this can also appear as **Alt text**).

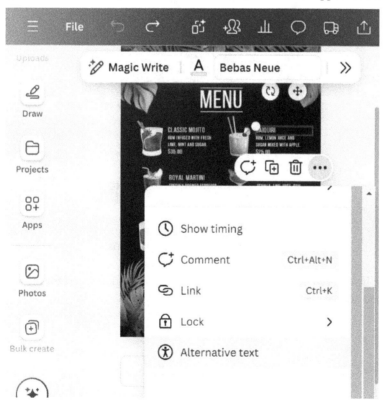

Figure 9.7: Finding the Alt text option

3. A pop-up window will appear where you can enter your alt text. Here are some tips for writing effective alt text:

    - *Be descriptive*: Briefly describe the content and purpose of the image. What information does it convey?

    - *Focus on functionality*: If the image is a chart or graph, explain the data it represents.

    - *Keep it concise*: Aim for 125 characters or less to ensure compatibility with screen readers.

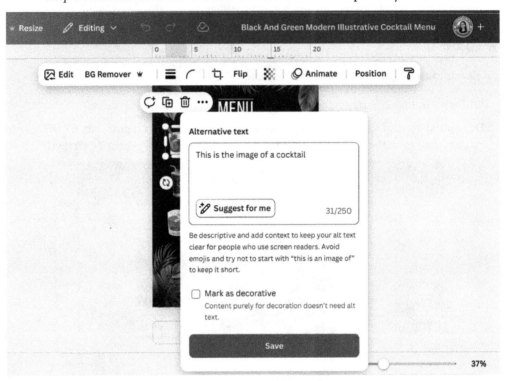

Figure 9.8: Adding alt text descriptions

    - *Use AI*: If you need help and have Canva Pro, you can click **Suggest for me** and Canva's AI will generate potential alt text for you.

- *Skip decorative elements*: Don't describe purely decorative images (e.g., patterns) unless they hold symbolic meaning. Simply check the **Mark as decorative** option instead.

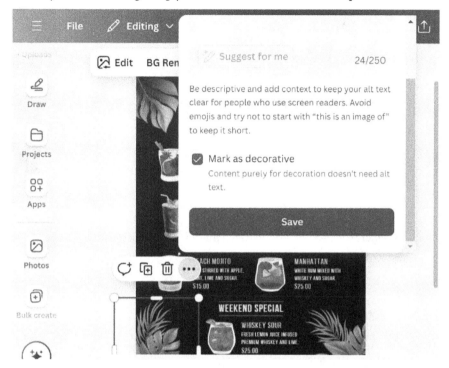

Figure 9.9: The Mark as decorative option

4. Once you've crafted your alt text, click **Save** to apply it to the image.

> **Bonus tip**
>
> Use keywords relevant to your content when appropriate, as they help your SEO if that design is posted on socia medial or on the internet. However, remember that although your brand positioning is surely very important for your business, smooth communication with your audience is too – so, always prioritize clarity over keyword stuffing.

There's more...

Social networks such as Facebook or LinkedIn allow you to add alt text directly from their internal editors. When you are uploading your content on LinkedIn, for instance, the possibility to add an alt text appears, letting you type your descriptive text in a textbox. This is a good idea to leverage your content to make it accessible to anyone on social media.

Figure 9.10: Adding alt text within the LinkedIn content editor

Enabling captions on videos and audio

Back in *Chapter 6*, we looked at the difference between subtitles and captions:

- **Subtitles** are manually added text overlays that become part of the video file. These can be generated (and edited!) through Canva's **Subtitles** app. When you download a video with subtitles, the subtitles are embedded, ensuring they are visible on any device or platform where the video is played.

- **Captions** are automatically generated transcripts that appear when a video is played within the Canva platform. However, these captions are not embedded within the video file itself. As a result, when you download a video with captions from Canva, the captions will not be included. Captions can also not be edited if Canva misinterprets the audio and generates a mistake.

In *Chapter 6*, we focused on how to generate subtitles, but this time, we will focus on captions. Here, I'll show you how to add captions to your Canva videos, making them accessible to everyone, regardless of hearing ability. Whether someone is deaf or hard of hearing, in a loud environment, or simply prefers captions, you can ensure your message reaches a wider audience with clear and inclusive content.

How to do it...

To generate captions, follow these steps:

1. From the home page, click **Settings**. You can also click your profile picture and select **Settings**.

2. Under **Your account**, scroll down to the **Accessibility** section.

3. Switch the **Captions** toggle on. Canva will automatically save your preference.

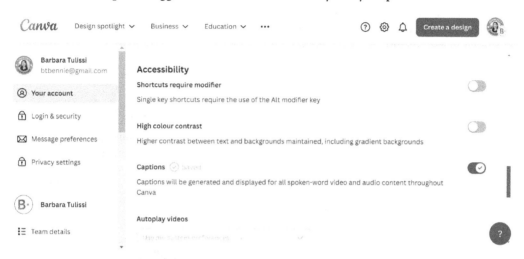

Figure 9.11: Enabling captions in the Accessibility panel

When you play back your videos, you will see the captions automatically added:

Figure 9.12: What captions look like

Now, when uploading a video, captions will be automatically shown.

> **Note**
>
> Remember that captions cannot be downloaded or edited since they are auto-generated. This means the relationship between the audio and the captions depends on the audio quality, which can result in spelling mistakes and errors.
>
> However, remember that subtitles can be edited. You can go back to *Chapter 6*, to the *Generating subtitles* recipe, for a reminder!
>
> It is also worth noting that the supported languages for captions are currently Arabic, Chinese (simplified), English (Australian), English (British), English (US), French, French (Canadian), German, Indonesian, Italian, Japanese, Korean, Portuguese (Brazilian), Spanish (US), Spanish (LATAM), Spanish (Spain), Thai, and Turkish. I sincerely believe new ones will be added very soon.

Creating images using AI

Ever envisioned an image that didn't quite exist in your library? Perhaps you sought a more diverse or inclusive representation, one that better reflects your brand or target audience. AI-generated images offer a creative solution to this challenge. While AI is a powerful tool, it's not without its limitations.

One significant concern is the potential for AI to perpetuate stereotypes. Algorithms trained on biased data can generate images that reinforce harmful stereotypes, particularly regarding race, gender, and ability. However, AI also has the potential to break down these stereotypes. By carefully curating training data and fine-tuning models, we can create AI systems that generate more accurate and inclusive representations.

To harness the power of AI while mitigating its risks, it's crucial to understand its limitations and use it responsibly. When working with AI-generated images, it's essential to do the following:

- *Review and edit*: Always carefully review AI-generated images for errors, inconsistencies, and biases

- *Diversify data*: Ensure that the AI models are trained on diverse and representative datasets to avoid perpetuating stereotypes

- *Human oversight*: Use human judgment to guide the AI process and ensure that the final output aligns with your desired vision

By following these guidelines, you can leverage AI to create innovative and inclusive visuals that empower your brand and resonate with your audience.

How to do it...

Let's try to overcome AI limitations and create an image with AI that could accurately represent inclusivity and diversity:

1. You can access **Magic Media** or **Magic Content** from the home page or inside the editor. To access it from the editor, select **Elements** and scroll until you find **AI image generator**. Then, click **Generate your own** to open the **Magic Media** panel.

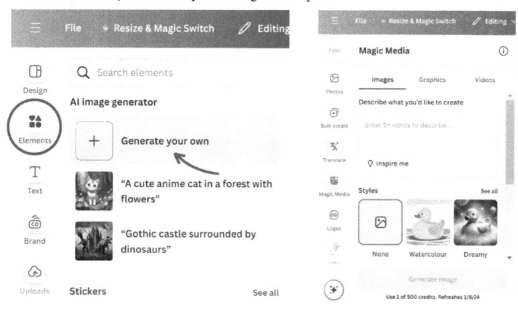

How to find it   *How it looks*

Figure 9.13: Finding the Magic Media feature

2. Under the **Images** tab, enter the description of the image you want – for instance, a `confident woman`. Remember to keep your prompt simple and concise since Canva AI is not capable of generating difficult output.

3.   Then, choose the style and aspect ratio that you want your AI image to be, and click **Generate image**.

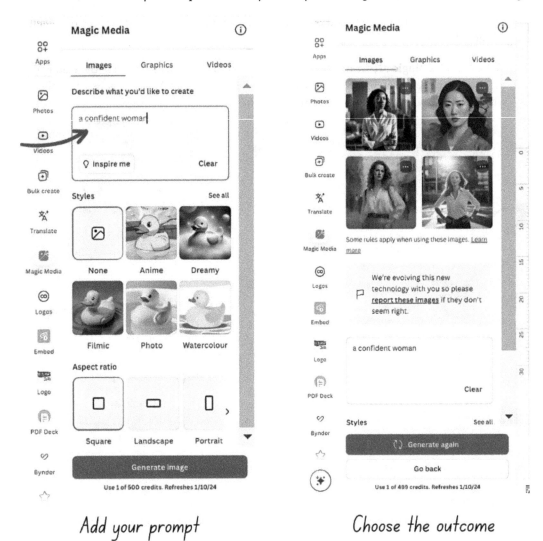

Add your prompt   Choose the outcome

Figure 9.14: Magic Media in action

4. You will now see some generated images:

    • To add the generated image to your design, simply click on the image

    • To create more images with the same prompt, select **Generate again**

    • If you'd like to generate more images similar to a specific image, click the three dots icon that appears while hovering over your preferred image and select **Generate more like this**

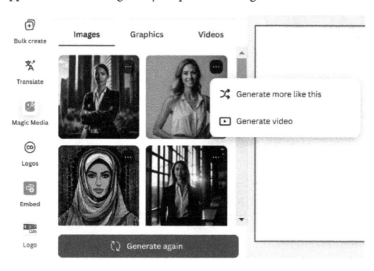

Figure 9.15: The Generate more like this option

Let's think about diversity and inclusivity. Looking at *Figure 9.14*, two of the generated images show white women and three of the images show business clothing. However, what about black women? Or Islamic women wearing sarees? They can represent confident women too. So, let's make our a confident woman prompt more specific. Inspired by Frida Kahlo's artistic passion, I imagine a strong, creative woman, painting in a colorful studio. While I'm not Hispanic, I resonate with her fearless creativity. To refine the prompt, click **Go back** and enter the new one instead, such as Hispanic woman creating her paintings in a colorful room. When you are happy with it, just click on your favorite image to add it to your design.

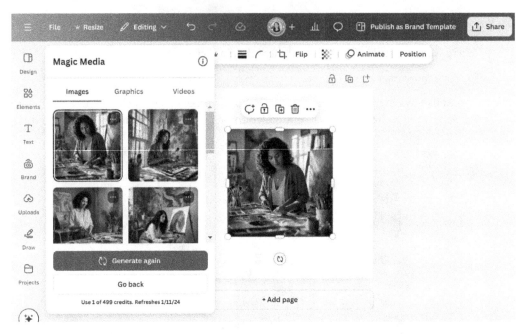

Figure 9.16: Generating an image of a Hispanic woman creating her paintings in a colorful room

> **Note**
>
> From October 2024, Podstock, a diverse media library championing representation, has been integrated into Canva. Now, you can easily access a wider range of stock photos featuring people from all walks of life. From race and gender to culture and ability, Podstock ensures that everyone feels seen and heard.

10

Designing Print-Ready Materials

Have you ever been thrilled with a Canva design, only to be disappointed by the final printed version? Don't worry, it happens to the best of us. Here's the thing: designing for screens and designing for print are two different games. This chapter will bridge that gap.

In this chapter, we'll explore the key adjustments needed to ensure your stunning Canva creations translate flawlessly onto flyers, brochures, or posters. We will discover the nuances of print design, learn how to convert pixel-based projects, and master the art of optimizing your designs for specific formats. By creating mock-ups, you will be a print-ready pro, confidently exporting high-quality designs that shine just as brightly on paper as they do on your screen.

In this chapter, we will cover the following recipes:

- Resizing your Canva project, ready for print
- Getting mock-ups for printing
- Using the Canva printing service
- Exporting your design as a PDF

Note

In this chapter, we will be working on a single project. Remember our meme from *Chapter 4*? Here, we will bring it to the material world!

Resizing your Canva project, ready for print

Ever dreamed of turning your digital masterpieces into tangible reality? Transforming your pixel-perfect designs into printed materials requires a strategic approach. While it might seem like a simple process, there are crucial considerations to ensure your printed creations meet your expectations.

In this recipe, we'll review some important considerations to keep in mind when designing a project for print, then look at how to resize the project – whether you are using a free or Pro version of Canva.

Getting ready

Here are some concepts you have to keep in mind before starting to design for print:

- **Millimeters and centimeters**: In the world of print, inches and pixels take a backseat, and millimeters and centimeters take to the stage. Here's why:

  - Printing relies on mechanical processes, and these machines operate best with well-defined, consistent units. Millimeters and centimeters offer a finer degree of control compared to inches, which can be less precise for detailed designs.

  - The printing industry is international, and centimeters are the standard unit of measurement in most countries. Using a universal system avoids confusion and ensures your design prints exactly as intended, no matter where it's produced.

  - Unlike pixels, which are fixed to screen resolution, millimeters and centimeters are adaptable. You can easily scale your design up or down without losing quality, making them perfect for projects of all sizes.

- **Color chameleon**: Those vibrant colors that pop on your screen use **red, green, and blue (RGB)** light. Print, however, relies on **cyan, magenta, yellow, and key-black (CMYK)** inks. This means those super-saturated tones might appear a bit muted or even off-color once printed.

- **Resolution reality check**: Screens can handle incredible detail, but printing has its limits. A design that looks sharp on your monitor could turn pixelated or blurry if not optimized for print.

Now, to follow along with this recipe (and the rest of the chapter), remember that we will be using the meme we created in *Chapter 4*.

How to do it...

Imagine that you love your meme so much that we want to print it – say, on a hoodie. How can we do it? To bridge the gap between digital design and printing it in Canva, we'll need to make some adjustments. Here's the deal with resizing your Canva project from social media to a hoodie:

- Social media graphics are typically designed for low resolutions on screens. Simply enlarging them for a hoodie might result in a pixelated, blurry mess.

- **Dots per inch** (**DPI**) determines image quality in print. Social media graphics usually have a low DPI, unsuitable for printing on fabric.

So, let's see how to resize the meme:

- If you have a free Canva account, follow these steps:

  I.   First, you need to know the measures of your current meme. To find this out, click **File**. Under the name of your project, you should see its size.

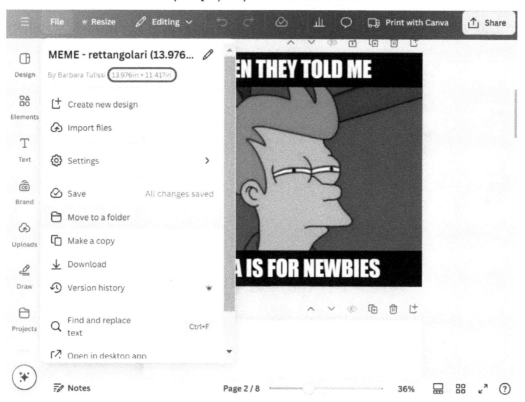

Figure 10.1: Finding your meme's size

II.   Open your internet browser and search `Google converter inches to millimeters`. A free converter will appear. This is just one of the many free online converters; you can use a different converter if you wish.

In graphic design, project size refers to the width and height of your design, written as "width x height" with the unit at the end (e.g., 13.976 in x 11.417 in). When using an online converter, enter these values one at a time – width first, then height – to get the equivalent measurements in millimeters. In our case, 13.976 in is equal to 354.9904 mm – but in Canva, we can approximate this measure to 355 mm.

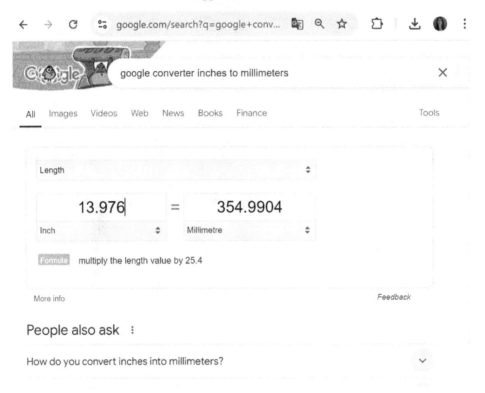

Figure 10.2: Using Google's free converter

III.   Go back to Canva, and from the dashboard, select **Custom size**.

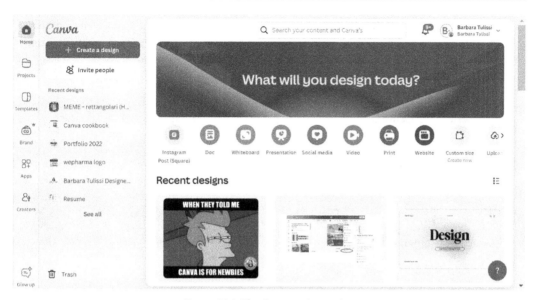

Figure 10.3: The Custom size option

IV.   In the **Custom size** window, enter the converted values. Just be careful to insert the right units!

Create a design   Custom size

✨ For you	
🗒 Docs	
🖼 Whiteboards	
🎴 Presentations	
💬 Social media	
🎬 Videos	
🖨 Print products	
🖥 Websites	
🗂 Custom size	
☁ Upload	
••• More	

Width: 355

Height: 290

Units: mm

Create new design

Suggested

🖼 Hoodie 355 × 290 mm

Figure 10.4: Custom size pop-up menu

V.   Once the new project has been opened, select your meme within your previous project, then copy and paste it into the new project. Since the previous project and the current one have the same dimensions, you won't need to make any adjustments.

- If you are a Canva Pro user, follow these steps:

    I.   With your Canva project open, click **Resize** in the top-left corner of the interface.

    II.   In the new panel, select **Custom size** to see the unit options.

    III.   To switch between measurement units, go to the **Units** drop-down menu and select **mm**. This will automatically convert your design's dimensions from inches to millimeters.

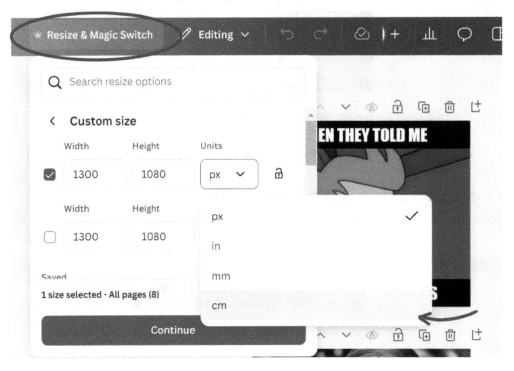

Figure 10.5: Resizing from inches to millimeters using Canva's Resize button

IV.   Once done, go to **File**, and under the project name, you can see the new dimensions:

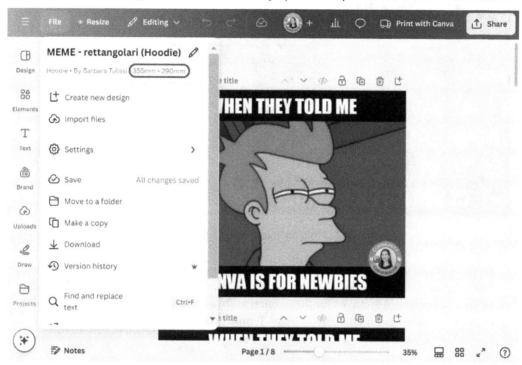

Figure 10.6: Our resized design

Now, check your image:

- First, I suggest manually checking if your image has a high resolution. You can zoom in using Canva's zoom option. While zooming in on an image in Canva can reveal pixelation, it's essential to access the level of detail at a realistic viewing distance. If the image appears blurry or grainy even when zoomed in moderately (around 200%), it's likely a sign of insufficient resolution. In the context of printing a meme on a hoodie, ensure the image is clear enough to maintain its quality when viewed up close.

Figure 10.7: Zooming in to check the resolution

- Secondly, if you have a Canva Teams subscription, I suggest activating the Template Assistant. The Template Assistant checks your designs for issues and suggests ways to fix them. Depending on your design type, it looks out for these concerns. To activate it in your project, go to the **File** menu, select **Settings**, and then select **Show Template Assistant**.

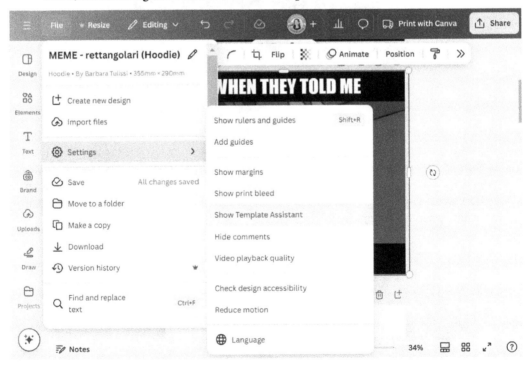

Figure 10.8: Finding the Template Assistant feature

When using Canva Pro, you'll notice that the Brand Kit feature is automatically enabled. This means that if your design deviates from your established brand guidelines, you may receive suggestions. Don't be alarmed! Canva's AI is working to ensure your designs remain consistent with your brand identity.

By following the Template Assistant's recommendations, you'll not only maintain brand consistency but also create visually appealing designs that translate well to print. The Template Assistant and Brand Kit work together to provide you with tailored suggestions and ensure your designs align with your brand's aesthetic.

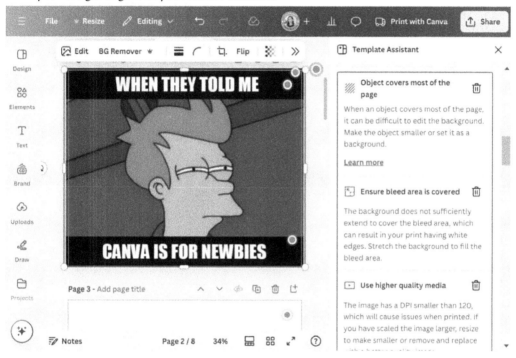

Figure 10.9: The Template Assistant panel

Getting mock-ups for printing

With the project completed and sized appropriately, you will now want to print it. But wait – wouldn't it be good if you could see what it will look like on our hoodie first? With Canva, you can easily make a printing mock-up.

In this recipe, we'll walk you through the process of creating a realistic mock-up, allowing you to visualize your design on a physical product before committing to print. This ensures you catch any design flaws and make necessary adjustments for optimal results.

How to do it...

There are actually two ways to get a mock-up in Canva – and this time, they have nothing to do with whether you're a free or Pro Canva user.

Method 1 – using the Mockups app

To use the Mockups app, follow these steps:

1. Download your meme as a .png or .jpg file, then upload it again in Canva's **Upload** section.
2. Within your meme project, add a new blank page.
3. Browse the **Apps** option. In the search bar, type Mockups and open the **Mockups** app.

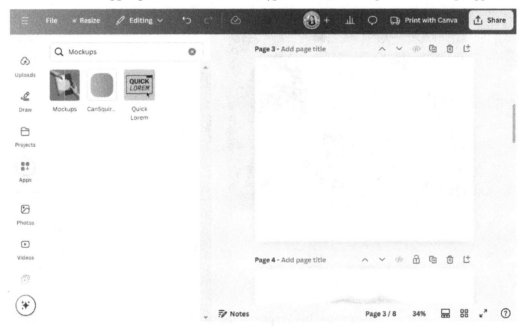

Figure 10.10: Finding the Mockups app

4. Since we are looking for a hoodie mock-up, we will navigate the **Apparel** section to find our favorite hoodie.

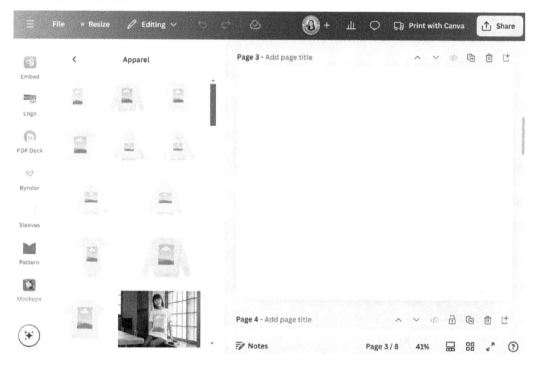

Figure 10.11: Searching for a hoodie mock-up

5. Once you have found the hoodie, drag and drop it onto your new blank page.

6.   Now a new panel will appear asking you to drag and drop the uploaded image into the mock-up. Do it and see the outcome!

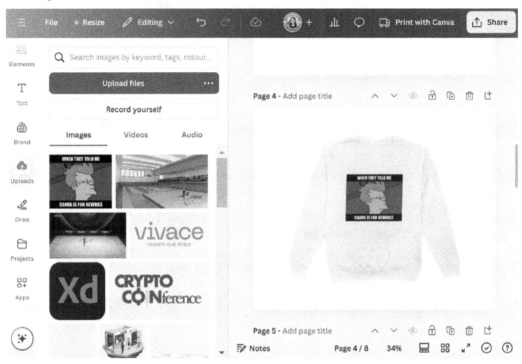

Figure 10.12: Dropping the meme onto the hoodie mock-up

Method 2 – using the Print with Canva button

When creating mock-ups using Canva's Mockups app, you have more flexibility in choosing the specific mock-up (for example, a hoodie, t-shirt, or hat). However, if you already start with a hoodie project, as we have done, you cannot choose a custom mock-up. But Canva still automatically generates a hoodie mock-up for you.

To see this mock-up, simply click on **Print with Canva**. In the new right-hand panel, you can use the expand arrow to enlarge the image and get a clearer idea of your printed outcome.

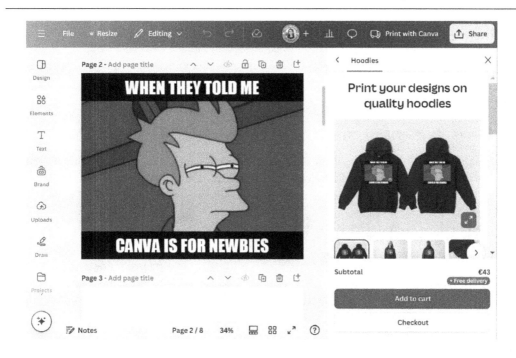

Figure 10.13: Canva's Print with Canva panel

Using the Canva Print service

Now that you know how your digital design will stay on your hoodie, let's print it. You don't even need to leave Canva for this – we can use Canva Print instead.

In this recipe, we'll see how to use Canva Print to guarantee a seamless transition from the digital realm to the physical world. Get ready to unleash your creativity and transform your designs into cherished keepsakes!

> **Note**
>
> Beyond delivering exceptional quality, Canva Print is committed to making a positive impact on the planet. By choosing Canva Print, you're not just getting stunning products; you're also supporting a company dedicated to sustainability.
>
> Canva actively offsets its carbon footprint by planting trees for every order placed. They also partner with eco-friendly suppliers, minimizing their environmental impact. Additionally, Canva promotes sustainable design practices, encouraging designers to create products that consider material usage and energy efficiency.
>
> By choosing Canva Print, you're not only getting high-quality products but also contributing to a greener future. Let's create beautiful designs together while making a positive difference for our planet!

Getting ready

To start, ensure you have your completed hoodie mock-up and meme design ready.

How to do it...

To use Canva Print, follow these steps:

1. With the meme project open, select **Print with Canva**. A panel will appear on the right, where you can customize your hoodie, before clicking **Add to cart**.

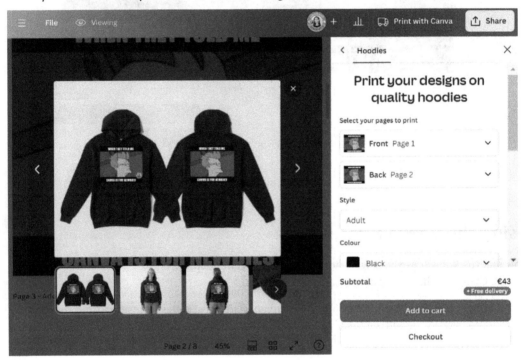

Figure 10.14: Hoodie options

2. Choose the design of the front and back of the hoodie. In our case, for **Front**, we can choose the page that contains our meme, and for **Back**, choose **None** to keep it blank.

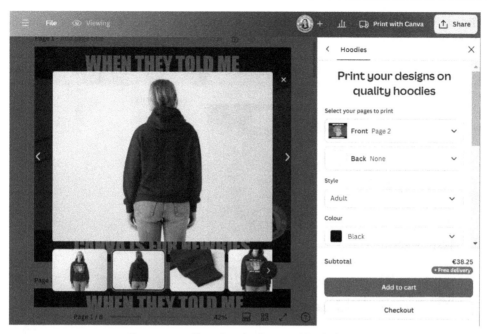

Figure 10.15: Choosing the front and back design

3.   Depending on your size, choose to purchase the hoodie for a toddler, a youth, or an adult.

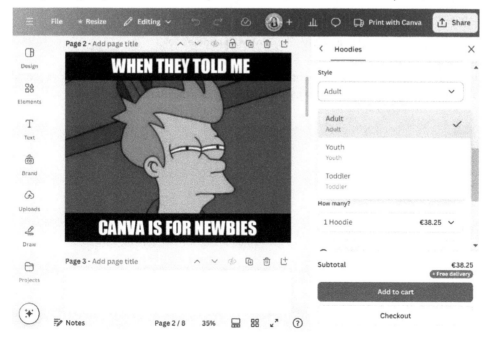

Figure 10.16: Choosing the hoodie's style

4. The choice of color depends a lot on the kind of apparel you choose. In the case of the hoodie, Canva currently gives just three options: black, gray, and navy. Choose the one you like the best.

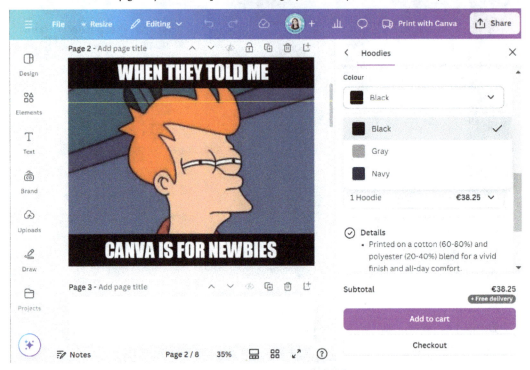

Figure 10.17: Choosing your hoodie's color

5. It's always difficult to choose the right size when purchasing apparel – that's why Canva provides a detailed size guide to avoid returns. Once ready, pick your size.

6. Then, you can choose the quantity – maybe you just want to purchase the hoodie for yourself, or for your teammates/fellow Canva-lovers too!

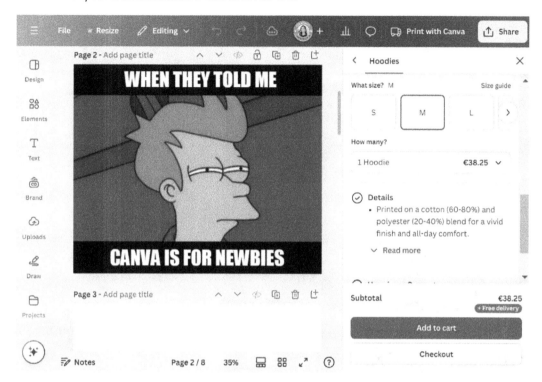

Figure 10.18: Choosing the hoodie's size

7. While in the **Details** section, Canva tells you some details about colors and materials used to print your order; in the **Happiness Guarantee** section, it notes that if you are not happy with your received order, you can talk with support to get it fixed or get a refund. You can read this information but don't need to actually do anything here.

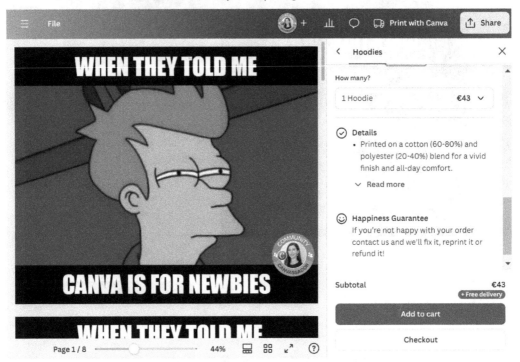

Figure 10.19: The Canva Print's Details and Happiness Guarantee section

8. Once you have gone through the options, select **Add to cart** and head to the checkout.

    The checkout will automatically show your shipping details based on those in your Canva account settings. If you have Canva Pro, it will also automatically show your chosen payment method; otherwise, it will ask you to add a payment method.

9. When you're ready, hit **Place order**!

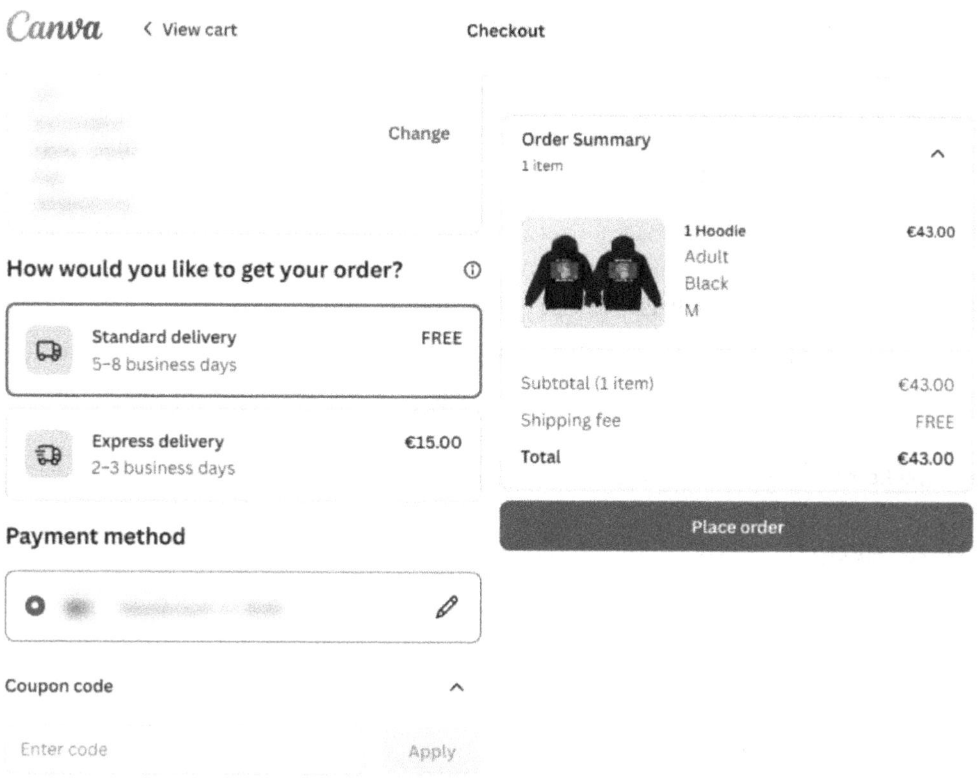

Figure 10.20: Complete the order

Exciting note!

Can't wait to get your hands on your Canva Print order? Well, expect a delightful surprise when your package arrives! Your custom creations will be nestled in an adorable, branded Canva box, showcasing their commitment to quality. Inside, you will find your stunning prints; plus, sometimes, Canva likes to provide some extra swag, such as stickers and discount codes – these extras are Canva's way of thanking you for choosing Canva Print.

Exporting your design as a PDF

In the previous recipe, we looked at how we can use Canva Print to print our designs. However, you may want to print the image yourself or send it to a different professional printing service. In this case, you will want to know how to export your design as a PDF.

You may be thinking that exporting the design as a PDF is an odd choice. Wouldn't an image format such as PNG or JPEG be better?

While PNG and JPEG are popular image formats, they have limitations when used for printing. PNG, despite its ability to cause compression, can introduce color shifts when converted to CMYK. JPEG, on the other hand, can suffer from quality degradation due to lossy compression.

For optimal print results, PDFs offer superior color accuracy, better control over image quality, and compatibility with various printing devices. By choosing PDF, you ensure your designs are printed precisely as intended.

So, now you know why we are choosing PDFs. Ready to dive in?

Getting ready

Bring along your resized meme from the previous recipe!

How to do it...

To export your project as a PDF, follow these steps:

1. Click the **Share** button in the top-right corner of the editor. Then, from the drop-down menu, select **Download**.

2. The **Download** settings panel will open. Under the **File type** dropdown, you can pick the file type that you want to download the project using.

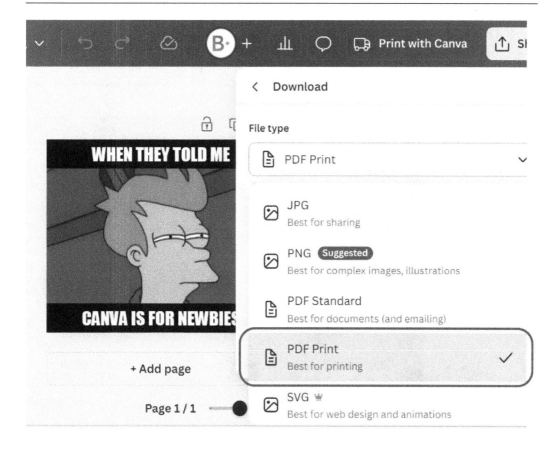

Figure 10.21: Finding the PDF Print option

Choose **PDF Print**. This option ensures your design is optimized for high-quality printing.

3. There are some options under the **File type** box that should be considered too:

    *   **Crop marks and bleed**: If you plan to use a professional printing service, consider enabling the **Crop marks and bleed** checkbox. This adds markers to guide precise trimming and a slight extension of your design to avoid white edges after cutting (bleed).

    *   To see the white edges before printing, go to **File | Settings** and check **Show print bleed**. A dashed line will show you the safe margin of your design. Beyond that line, the extra area will be cut in the printing process.

- **Flatten PDF**: Why should you flatten your PDF? Because PDFs can have hidden layers, tricky transparencies, and exotic fonts. Flattening merges layers, converts transparency to printer-friendly formats, embeds fonts as images, and removes unsupported features. This creates a universal PDF for any printer to understand and ensures your document prints exactly as intended.

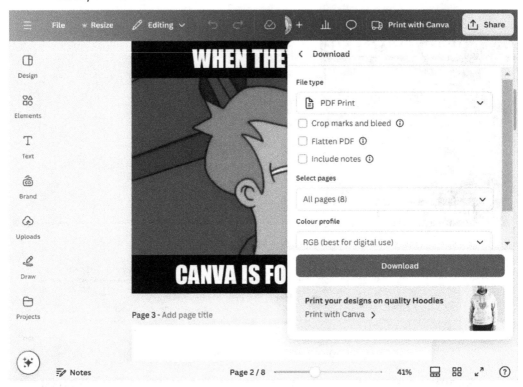

Figure 10.22: The Crop marks and bleed option and the Flatten PDF option

- **Include notes**: Leaving a note for the printer is like sending a friendly message alongside your design. It clarifies details such as double-sided printing or paper type, highlights crucial info on bleed marks or color profiles, and even explains unique folds or layouts for complex prints. This little note goes a long way in ensuring your creation looks exactly as intended.

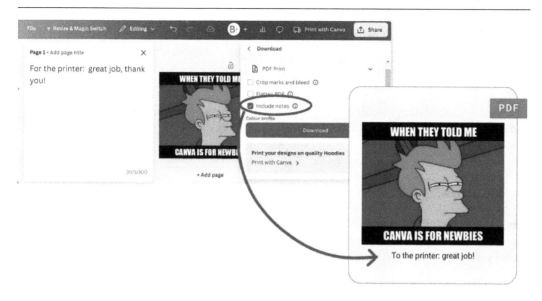

Figure 10.23: The Include notes option

- **Color profile**: Printers use CMYK inks to create colors, while screens display them in RGB. CMYK has a smaller color range (gamut) than RGB. So, some vibrant RGB colors that you might see on Canva might not be perfectly reproduced with CMYK inks. Converting beforehand lets you adjust for this limitation and get a predictable output.

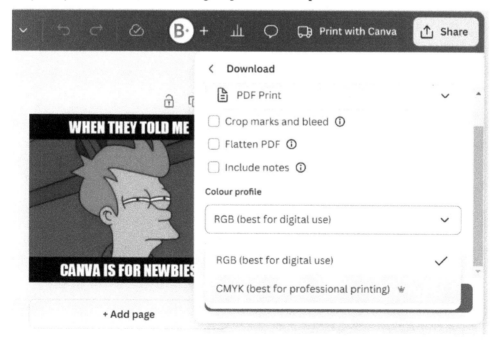

Figure 10.24: The Colour profile option

4. Once done, click the **Download** button to initiate the download process. Then, open the downloaded PDF file and send it to your printer or upload it to a printing service's platform.

> **Tip**
>
> For professional printing, consider using Canva Pro or Canva Teams, which offer additional options such as CMYK color mode (better suited for printing compared to RGB) for even more control over the final output.

There's more...

Before committing to a full print run, you should always conduct a thorough proofreading process. By carefully reviewing your PDF design, you can identify and correct any errors or inconsistencies, ensuring your printed material meets your highest standards.

When printing the image, set the printing scale so that your design gets printed in the correct size.

Then, take the time to evaluate the overall quality, readability, and visual appeal of your design. Check for font clarity, image resolution, and margin alignment. This will help you avoid costly reprints and ensure your final product is a reflection of your vision.

11
Unlocking the Power of Magic Studio

Imagine having a personal design assistant that could instantly transform your ideas into stunning visuals. That's the power of Canva's Magic Studio. This innovative tool empowers you to create original images and videos with just a simple description. No longer are you limited by your design skills or the time it takes to create complex visuals. With Magic Studio, inspiration can be brought to life in a matter of minutes.

But that's not all. Magic Studio also offers a transformative feature that can breathe new life into your existing designs. Simply upload your work, and let the tool suggest new styles, colors, and layouts. It's like having a designer's touch at your fingertips.

Why is this so important for digital marketers, designers, and social media managers? The answer lies in the efficiency and creativity that Magic Studio brings to the table. By automating certain aspects of the design process, you can save valuable time and focus on other essential tasks. Moreover, Magic Studio can inspire new ideas and help you experiment with different styles without the fear of starting from scratch.

In essence, Canva's Magic Studio is a game-changer that can elevate your design capabilities. Whether you're a seasoned professional or just starting out, this powerful tool can help you achieve your creative goals and create visuals that truly stand out.

So, in this chapter, we will cover the following recipes:

- Transforming your pictures with Magic Edit
- Removing backgrounds
- Grabbing objects within a picture
- Erasing objects within a picture
- Expanding your pictures
- Resizing your content
- Generating brand-new illustrations with AI
- Writing with AI
- Extracting text from images
- Extracting video highlights
- Transforming existing elements
- Animating your designs

Useful resources

Grab this workbook, which will walk you through Canva's AI features, explaining what they do and where to find them: `https://partner.canva.com/LXb360`.

Note

If you are a free Canva user, you won't have access to the Pro features; however, you can still experience the magic during Canva's promotional periods. This allows you to try out the features with a limited number of uses. Keep an eye out for these opportunities! You can also check this link for potential promotions: `https://partner.canva.com/Gmz3Mr`.

Transforming your pictures with Magic Edit (Free)

Ever wanted to do a complex edit, but never had the time or resources? Canva's AI-powered photo editor has your back, transforming your photos with Magic Edit. Using the AI prompt, you can add anything to your design: clouds, mountains, roses – honestly, anything! Let your imagination run wild, and turn text prompts into effortless edits with AI image editing.

How to do it...

Here's how to use Magic Edit:

1. Select your image, click **Edit image**, and select **Magic Edit**.

Figure 11.1: Finding Magic Edit

2. Use the **Brush** or **Click** tool to select the image you want to transform.

> **Note**
>
> I suggest using the **Brush** tool when working with a device that allows you to select the area you want to edit with your fingertips – this gives you more freedom to draw the area in a more custom way. Otherwise, I suggest using the **Click** function, which works just as well.

3. Add a prompt in the **Describe your edit** field.

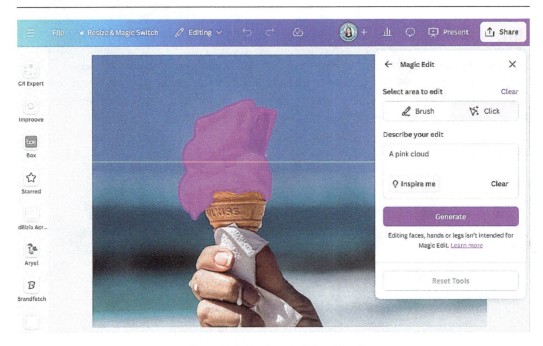

Figure 11.2: Brush and click options

4. Once done, click the **Generate** button. Then watch as Magic Edit transforms your image – in my case, my ice cream has transformed into a pink cloud:

Figure 11.3: Magic Edit in action – from ice cream to cloud

Remember that it can sometimes take more than just one generation to get the result you need – you can click **Generate again** or change the prompt completely. Here, I have changed the ice cream cloud to one that looks like a bouquet of flowers:

Figure 11.4: Magic Edit in action – from ice cream cloud to flower bouquet

Removing backgrounds (Pro)

Need a quick headshot for your CV or a custom photo for tomorrow's class presentation? The image background remover on Canva speeds up the editing process by instinctively detecting the foreground in your photo, so you can focus on what matters most.

How to do it...

Here's how to remove a background:

1. Upload your image, making sure it is a `.jpg`, `.png`, `.heic`, or `.heif` file (or even a stock image from the Canva library).

2. Then select your image and click **BG Remover** on the edit bar.

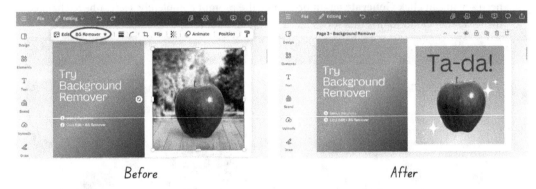

Before   After

Figure 11.5: Background Remover before and after

3. If you want to download your transparent background image, click **Share | Download**. Then, from the **Download** panel, for **File type**, choose **PNG**, and check the **Transparent background** option.

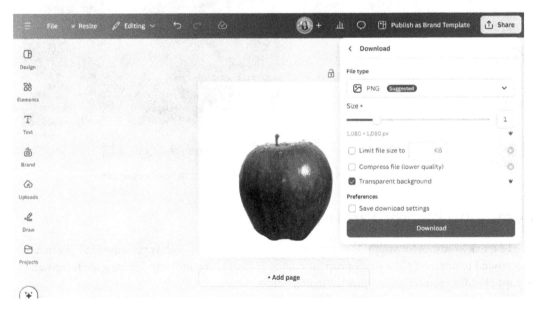

Figure 11.6: Download your image with a transparent background

> **Note**
>
> If you are looking for a free alternative, you can go to `https://www.remove.bg/` (we saw this back in *Chapter 3*, in the *Improving your profile picture* recipe).

Grabbing objects within a picture (Pro)

Need to tweak elements in your pictures? Well, Magic Grab isolates all the elements of your photo – the subject, the objects in the foreground, the items in the background – so you can simply click, then edit, resize, and reposition them individually.

How to do it...

Here's how to use Magic Grab:

1. Select your image, then click **Edit image** | **Magic Grab**.

Figure 11.7: Finding Magic Grab

2. From there, you can select the object you want to grab – in my case, using the **Brush** tool will give me more freedom when drawing on the astronaut, but I could use the **Click** tool too.

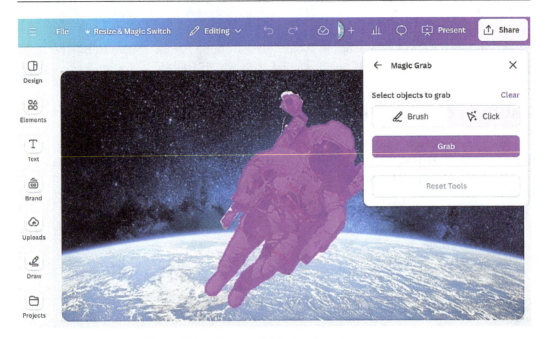

Figure 11.8: Using the click feature to grab the image

3.   Once selected, click on **Grab** to make the change definitive. In my case, I can now move the astronaut onto the moon.

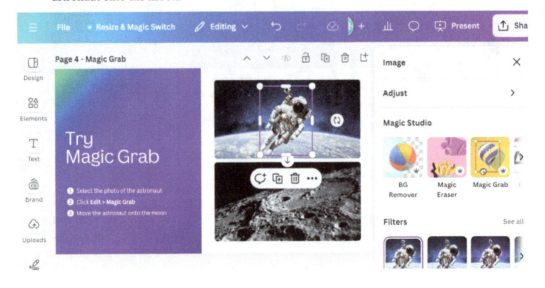

Figure 11.9: Making the astronaut float from space to the moon

Erasing objects within a picture (Pro)

We've just seen how to move objects with Magic Grab, but what about erasing images? Well, say goodbye to endless hours of manual editing with Magic Eraser. Magic Eraser uses its AI smarts to effortlessly remove unwanted backgrounds from your photos. Now, you can seamlessly place your subject on a new background or create stunning clean cutouts.

How to do it...

Here's how to use Magic Eraser:

1. Select your image, click **Edit image**, then click **Magic Eraser**.

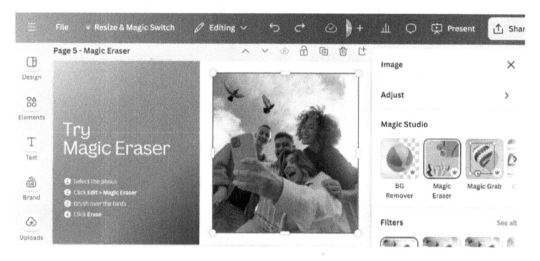

Figure 11.10: Finding Magic Eraser

2. Select the object you want to grab by drawing with the **Brush** option on it (or just using the **Click** function). In this case, I will select the birds.

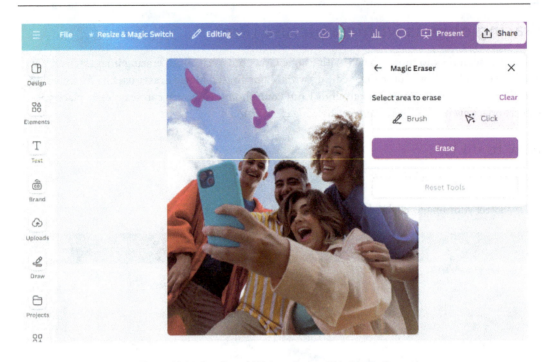

Figure 11.11: Brush and Click options within Magic Eraser

3.   Once the object is selected, click **Erase**. The object will be deleted from the image:

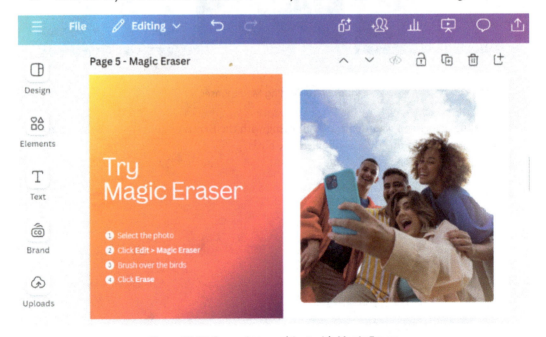

Figure 11.12: Removing an object with Magic Eraser

Expanding your pictures (Pro)

Magic Expand seamlessly extends an image in any direction to get the perfect shot. In seconds, you can fill in the rest of your image and generate the missing details. From social media to marketing campaigns, use our AI picture expander to enrich your visual content—with quality and detail intact. As a plus, it fixes awkward framing, saves zoomed-in images, or turns a vertical shot into a horizontal one in seconds.

How to do it...

Here's how to use Magic Expand:

1. Select your image in your Canva project, click **Edit image**, then **Magic Expand**.

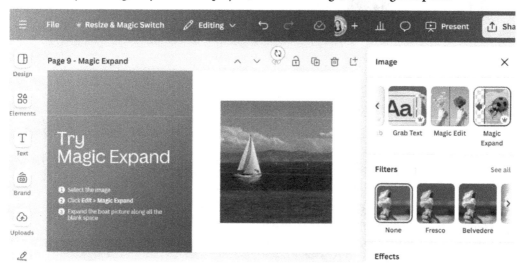

Figure 11.13: Finding Magic Expand

2. Navigate to the **Crop** tab. Under the **Expand** option, pick your desired aspect ratio. Here, we have clicked **Freeform**.

3. Then click **Magic Expand** to magically extend your image with AI.

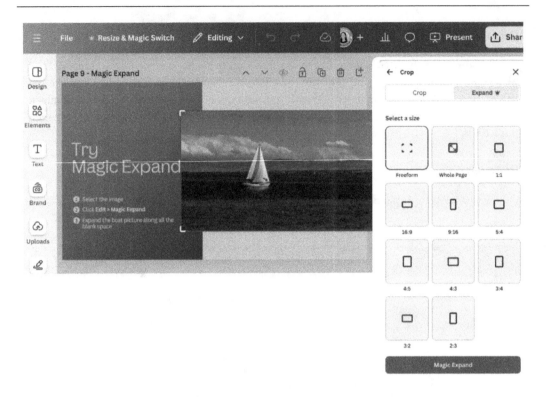

Figure 11.14: Freeform expand option within Magic Expand

4. If you are not happy with the expansion format, you can always select another format and click **Magic Expand** again. Here, we have changed the image to the **9:16** format.

Figure 11.15: Expand your image in the 9:16 vertical format

Resizing your content (Pro)

Need your content for different platforms, but don't have time to resize it manually? That's where the **Resize** AI tool comes in. This can be really handy when adapting content for different social media platforms. Let's discover how you can speed up your crafting process with this powerful tool.

How to do it...

Here's how to use **Resize**:

1. Open up your Canva project – in my case, I am working on a presentation.

2. Locate **Resize** on the top bar of Canva's project interface.

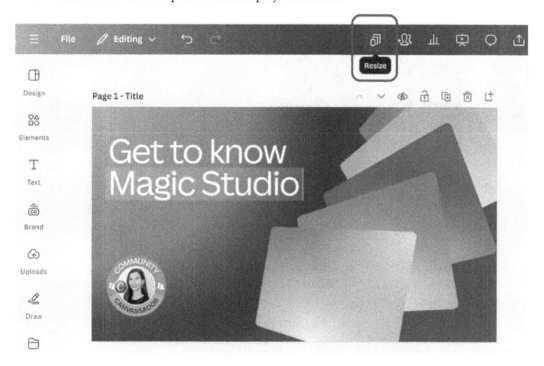

Figure 11.16: Finding the Resize option within our presentation

3. From the menu, click the format you want to resize the project in, for example, **Document (A4 Portrait)**.

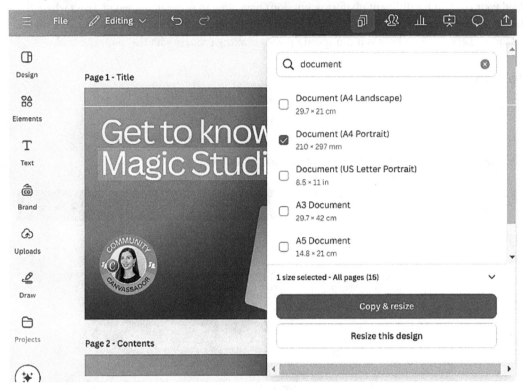

Figure 11.17: Choosing the new size

4. You can choose whether to resize the current project or to create a copy of the original one. Choose the best option for your needs. Once resized, you will need to fix some parts of the design to make it fit the new size.

Figure 11.18: Our presentation resized into a document

Generating brand-new illustrations with AI (Pro)

While we explored the capabilities of Magic Media in *Chapter 9*, there's a hidden gem within this powerful tool: the ability to generate illustrations. While creating pictures and videos is undoubtedly impressive, illustrations offer a unique advantage.

Unlike pictures generated by AI, which can often be easily recognized, illustrations can blend seamlessly into human-created artwork. Their non-photorealistic nature makes it more challenging to discern whether they were generated by AI. This is particularly beneficial for those seeking original and visually striking designs that don't raise eyebrows.

So, if you're looking to create illustrations that are both visually appealing and indistinguishable from human-made artwork, Magic Media is the tool for you.

How to do it...

Here's how to use Magic Media:

1. Open up a generic Canva project.
2. Click **Elements** from the sidebar, scroll down, and click **AI image generator**.
3. From there, select the **Generate your own** option.

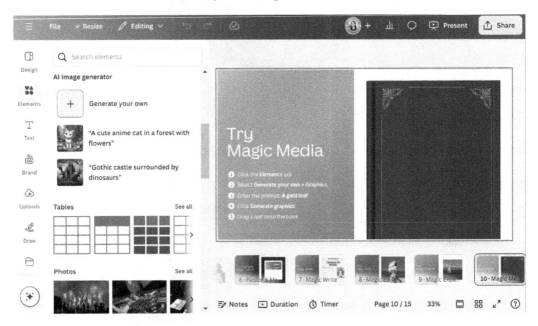

Figure 11.19: Finding Magic Media in the Elements panel

4. Open the **Graphics** tab, which is the one that allows you to create illustrations:

Figure 11.20: Magic Media Graphics tab

5. In its prompt bar, describe the illustration you'd like to generate – the more detail you can provide, the better. I have simply gone for golden leaf.

6. You can also choose an illustration style from the available options, such as **3D chrome**, **Doodle**, **Hand drawn**, or **Sticker**. I usually like to select **None**, to let Magic Media generate results with no specific style.

7. Then, click **Generate graphics**. Every generation will give you four outcomes, but if you do not like any of them you can simply click **Generate again**.

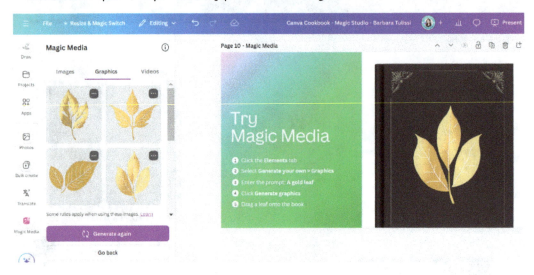

Figure 11.21: Magic Media's outcomes

Writing with AI (Pro)

Magic Write is the Canva feature that allows you to go from a prompt to a first draft or on-brand copy in no time using this AI tool. You can use it to write anything from social media captions to profile bios to brainstorming and seeking inspiration for poems or letters with one simple prompt. You can also use Magic Write to edit your existing draft — ask Magic Write to summarize, reword, expand, or make your work more fun or formal.

How to do it...

Here's how to use Magic Write:

1. Open a Canva project that contains text.
2. Click on one of the textboxes and you will see the **Magic Write** option appear in the top menu.

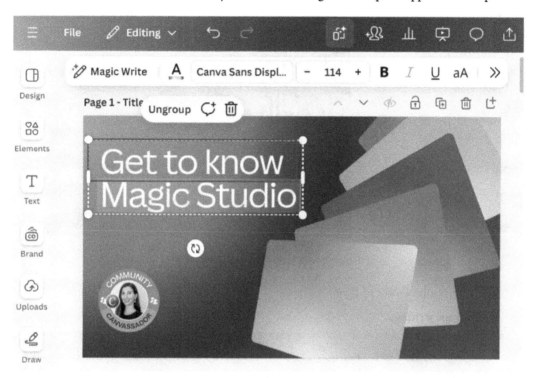

Figure 11.22: Finding Magic Write

3.   From the list, choose the Magic Write feature you want to use:

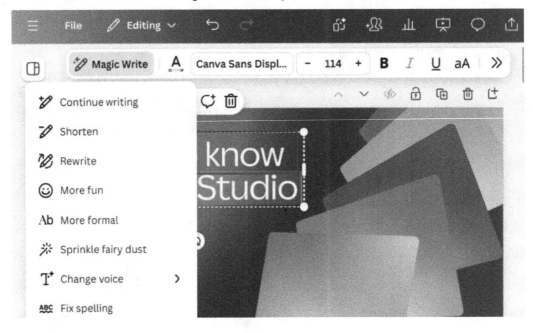

Figure 11.23: Magic Write options

Here's the result of some of them:

- **Continue writing**:

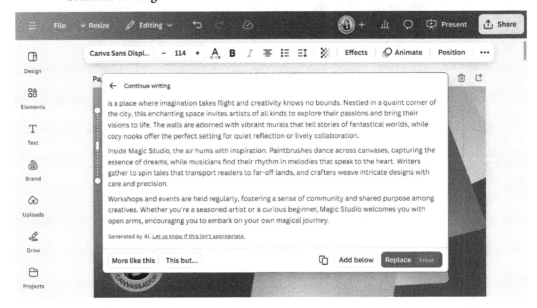

Figure 11.24: How Continue writing works

- **More fun**:

Figure 11.25: How More fun works

- **Sprinkle fairy dust**:

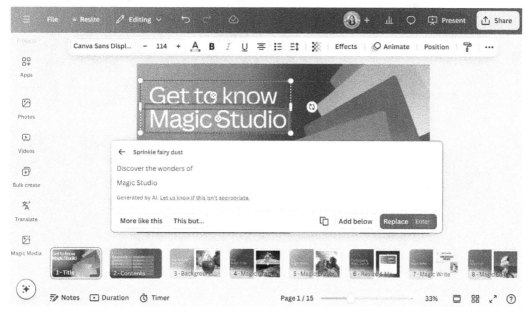

Figure 11.26: How Sprinkle fairy dust works

Test each option out and see which one works best for what you want/need!

Extracting text from images (Pro)

Imagine having the ability to extract text from images and seamlessly edit it to match your design vision. With **Grab Text**, this is no longer a dream. This powerful tool allows you to effortlessly transform text within images, giving you complete control over the font, size, and color.

No more struggling with manual text extraction or copying and pasting. **Grab Text** simplifies the process, saving you time and effort while ensuring your designs look professional and polished.

How to do it...

Here's how to use **Grab Text**:

1. Open up a Canva project and choose an image containing some text.

2. Then, to find **Grab Text**, select your image, click **Edit image**, then **Grab Text**.

Figure 11.27: Finding Grab Text

3. Click **Grab**. Once Canva has detached your text from the image, you can move it around or just change it.

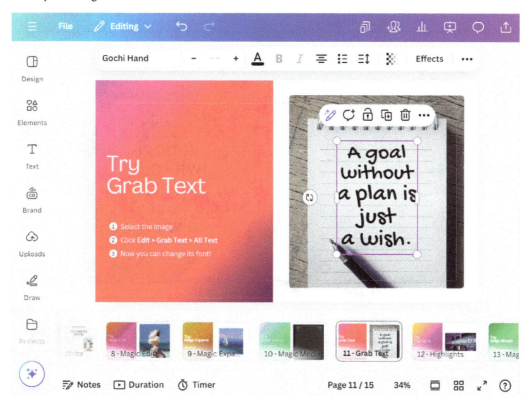

Figure 11.28: Isolating/grabbing the text and detaching it from the image

4. Let's suppose we want to change the font to Roboto. We can do it by clicking the font's current name in the toolbar and searching for Roboto.

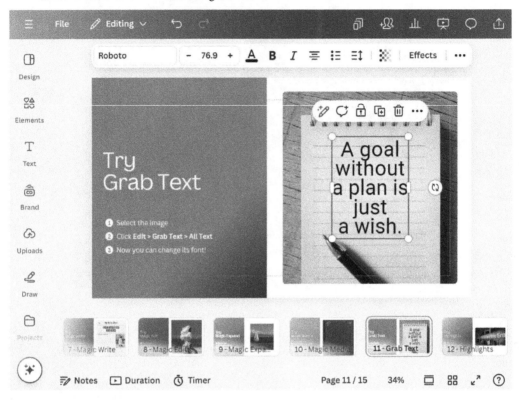

Figure 11.29: Changing the font to Roboto

Extracting video highlights (Pro)

Are you struggling to keep your audience engaged with lengthy videos? Canva Highlights is the solution you've been waiting for. This innovative feature automatically analyzes your videos and extracts the most captivating moments, creating engaging clips that are perfect for sharing on social media or incorporating into other projects.

How to do it...

Here's how to use Canva Highlights:

1. Open a Canva project and upload a custom video or choose one from the Canva library.
2. Select your video. Then, in the editor toolbar, click on the **Edit** button or on the scissors icon to unveil the trimming option.

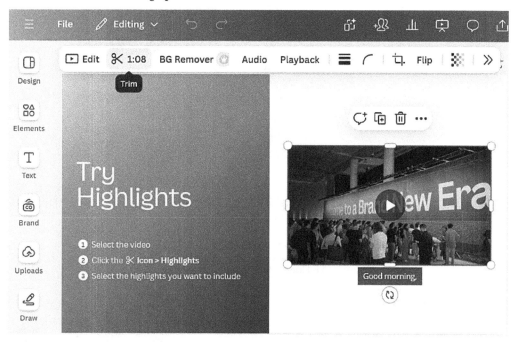

Figure 11.30: Finding the Trim option in the toolbar

3. Then, from the new toolbar, click the **Highlights** feature.

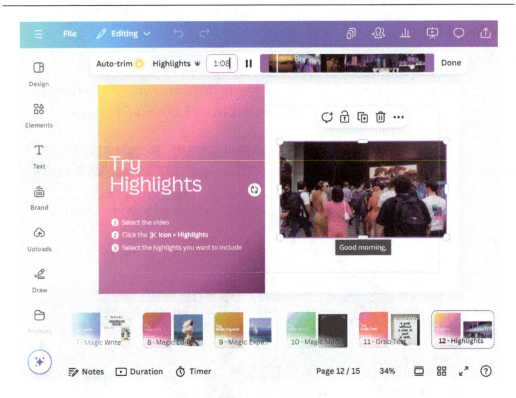

Figure 11.31: Finding the Highlights feature

4.   From the panel, choose your favorite clip to be added to your design.

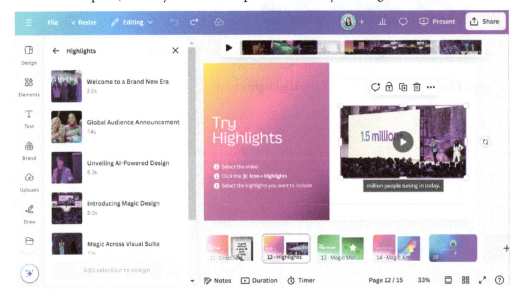

Figure 11.32: Choosing your favorite clip

Transforming existing elements (Free)

Imagine having the power to transform simple text or shapes into visually stunning elements with just a few words. That's the magic of Magic Morph. This innovative Canva app allows you to effortlessly apply effects, patterns, and textures to your designs, turning ordinary elements into extraordinary creations.

How to do it...

Here's how to use Magic Morph:

1. Open your Canva project, click **App** from the left-hand menu, and find the **Magic Morph** app.

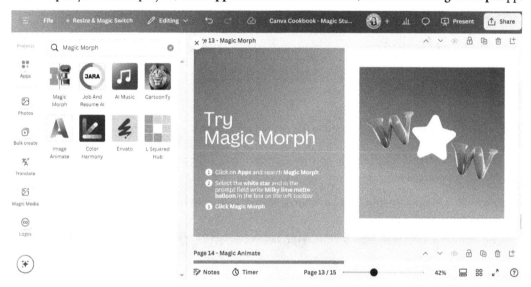

Figure 11.33: Finding the Magic Morph app

2. With the **Magic Morph** app open, select the object you want to transform within your design (it can be text or another element).

3. Then, in the prompt field, type the outcome you want – I want to transform my star into what I am describing as a `milky lime matte balloon`.

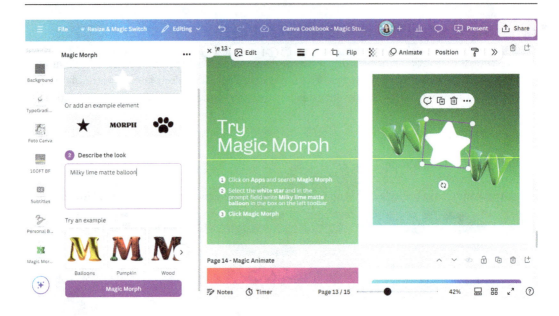

Figure 11.34: Generating the desired effect from the prompt bar

You can also try with a premade prompt suggested below the prompt bar: **Balloon**, **Pumpkin**, **Wood**, **Flowers**, and so on.

4. Now click **Magic Morph**. You can choose from the various outcome results or click **Create again** for more results.

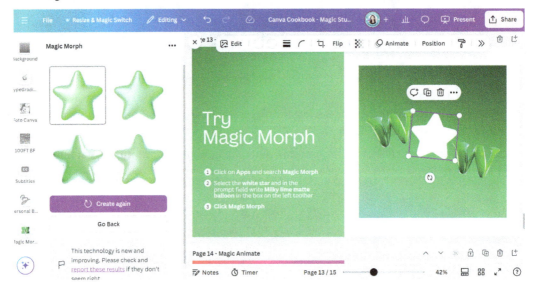

Figure 11.35: Final results of Magic Morph

Animating your designs (Pro)

Tired of spending hours manually selecting and positioning animations and transitions? Magic Animate is the solution you've been waiting for. This powerful Canva feature uses AI to automatically add animations to your entire design, saving you time and effort, especially for longer presentations and videos.

Getting ready

Open the workbook link provided at the start of the chapter: https://partner.canva.com/ LXb36o

How to do it...

Here's how to use Magic Animate:

1. From the workbook link, go to the last slide.
2. Click on the slide background, then go to the editor toolbar, and click **Animate**.
3. From here, animation options will show on the side panel, including **Magic Animate**.

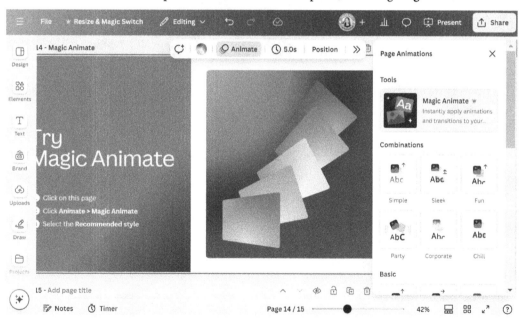

Figure 11.36: Finding Magic Animate

4. Once selected, you can choose the recommended style to apply to your entire design or an alternative one. In this case, the recommended style is **Digital**, which uses a mixture of slide-in and glitch animations. However, if you want to give your presentation a more corporate feeling, then you can use the **Professional** animation. Or, if you want to make it less animated and more focused on certain elements, you can apply a **Minimalistic** animation instead. I encourage you to hover with your mouse over the different animations to get a realistic preview of the final outcome once applied.

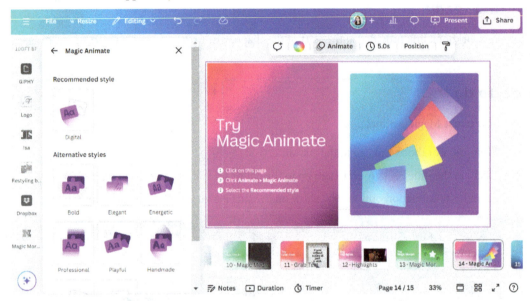

Figure 11.37: Picking up a style

5. If you do not like any of the preset animations, just click **Remove Magic Animation** to remove it from your entire design.

Index

A

ad
 formats, tailoring for different
  platforms 178-184
 objective, identifying 174, 175
 target audience, identifying 174, 175
AI
 used, for creating images 236-240
 writing with 282-285
AI-generated images
 essentials 236
alt text
 using, for images and graphics 231-233
animated swipe-bounce effect
 creating, for carousel 84-86
animation presentation
 considerations 124
 Element Animations 119
 Page Animations 118, 119
 transitions, adding between slides 120-122
 utilizing 117, 123

B

backgrounds (Pro)
 removing 269-271
Beat Sync 157
brand
 creating 18
 mission 21-24
 scope 19, 20
 values 24-28
 vision 20
brand archetype
 creating 28-31
Brand Hub 6-8, 42-47
brand-new illustrations, with AI (Pro)
 generating 279-281
brand's tone, of voice
 crafting 50-53

brand visual identity, in Canva
Brand Hub 42-47
colors 34-38
developing 32
elements 34
fonts 38-41
icons 41, 42
illustrations 41, 42
images 41, 42
mood board 32, 33

C

calls to action (CTAs) 78, 173
creating, tips 197, 198
utilizing, effectively 195-197
Canva
external resources, incorporating 12-15
interfaces, discovering 2
project, resizing 242-249
search bar 3
templates 4, 5
upload limits, reviewing 12-15
used, for exporting presentations 133, 134
used, for importing presentations 131-133
used, for sharing presentations 134, 135
useful shortcuts, implementing 16
Canva Free
color box 74
Mood board tab 74
single post tab 74
Canva Highlights
used, for extracting video
    highlights (Pro) 288-290
Canva, interface
Brand Hub 6-8
design button, creating 11, 12
search bar 3

single project interface 9, 10
templates 4, 5
Visual Suite 4
Canva presentation
presenting 124-129
Canva Print service
using 253-258
Canva Pro 76, 77, 157
Canva's video AI
working with 170, 171
CapCut
creating 168, 169
captions 158
enabling, on videos and audio 234-236
carousels 78
animated swipe-bounce effect,
    creating 84-86
call to action (CTA) 78
content slides 78
cover slide 78
hook slide 78
seamless carousels 79-83
slide carousels 79-82
centimeters 242
client presentation
creating 97-102
reviewing 107
collage post layout
creating 86, 87
color chameleon 242
content (Pro)
resizing 277, 278
content slides 78
cover slide 78
**cyan, magenta, yellow, and
    key-black (CMYK) 242**

D

data visualization 109-112
design
    animating 293, 294
    button, creating 11, 12
    exporting, as PDF 260-264
digital business card
    creating 200-204
document presentation
    creating 107, 108
dots per inch (DPI) 243

E

Element Animations 119
email signature
    creating 216-221
event flyer
    areas, of improvement 206
    transforming 204-212

F

Facebook
    profile, personalizing 65, 66
    social covers, designing 63-65

G

GIFs
    creating 161-164
Google Ads 175
Grab Text
    used, for extracting text from
        images (Pro) 286-288
graphic design
    best practices 225, 226

H

hook slide 78

I

images
    captions, with AI 236-240
images and graphics
    alt text, using for 231-233
infographics presentation
    layout, finding 116
    using 112-115
Instagram
    mosaic effect, creating 88, 89
Instagram grid mockup
    creating 56-61
    customizing 62, 63

L

label
    creating 164-167
Layouts feature 103-106
LinkedIn
    banner, creating 67, 68
    social covers, designing 63-65

M

Magic Animate
    used, for animating designs (Pro) 293, 294
Magic Edit (Free)
    used, for transforming pictures 267-269
Magic Eraser
    used, for erasing objects withing
        pictures (Pro) 273, 274

Magic Expand
   used, for expanding pictures (Pro) 275, 276
Magic Grab
   used, for grabbing objects withing
      pictures (Pro) 271, 272
Magic Media
   used, for generating brand-new
      illustrations with AI (Pro) 279-281
Magic Morph
   used, for transforming
      elements (Free) 291, 292
Magic Switch feature 107
Magic Write
   used, for writing with AI (Pro) 282-285
margins 72
meme generators
   reference link 96
memes 93
   creating 94-96
   resizing 243, 244
Meta Ads 175
Meta Ads Library 176, 177
millimeters 242
mockup 56
   app, using 250, 251
   obtaining 249
mood board 32, 33
mosaic effect
   creating, for Instagram 88, 89

N

near-field communication (NFC) 200

O

objects
   erasing, within picture (Pro) 273, 274
   grabbing, within picture (Pro) 271, 272
online advertising
   dos and don'ts 194, 195

P

Page Animations 118, 119
PDF
   design, exporting as 260-264
pictures
   expanding 276
   expanding, with Magic Expand 275
   objects, erasing within 273, 274
   objects, grabbing within 271, 272
   transforming, with Magic
      Edit (Free) 267-269
PineTools 83
   URL 89
presentations
   exporting, from Canva 133, 134
   importing, into Canva 131-133
   sharing, in Canva 134, 135
Print with Canva button
   using 252
profile picture
   improving 53-56

R

readable text and typography
   creating 225-230
red, green, and blue (RGB) 242
resolution reality check 242

S

seamless carousel 79-83

single project interface 9, 10

slide carousel
creating 79-82

social media post
taking, to next level 72-74

social media story 90, 91
creating 92

stealing like an artist method 73, 74

stellar reference materials
Meta Ads Library 176, 177
searching 175
strategic insights 177-178

stop-scrolling ads
crafting 184-194

subtitles
generating 158-160

swipe effect 84

T

template, for invoices and quotes
creating 213-216

text, from images (Pro)
extracting 286-288

V

video clips
editing, with Canva's AI 169-171

video highlights (Pro)
extracting 288-290

videos and audio
captions, enabling on 234-236

Visual Suite 4

W

Web Content Accessibility Guidelines (WCAG) 223
principles 224
requirements 224
reviewing 224

World Wide Web Consortium (W3C) 224

Y

Yoga Academy video
animating 150
animations, adding 150-153
creating 142-150
exporting 157
music, adding 155-157
previewing 157
purpose and message, defining 138-141
structuring 142-150
timings, setting 153-155

YouTube
banner, creating 69, 70
social covers, designing 63-65

packtpub.com

Subscribe to our online digital library for full access to over 7,000 books and videos, as well as industry leading tools to help you plan your personal development and advance your career. For more information, please visit our website.

Why subscribe?

- Spend less time learning and more time coding with practical eBooks and Videos from over 4,000 industry professionals

- Improve your learning with Skill Plans built especially for you

- Get a free eBook or video every month

- Fully searchable for easy access to vital information

- Copy and paste, print, and bookmark content

Did you know that Packt offers eBook versions of every book published, with PDF and ePub files available? You can upgrade to the eBook version at packtpub.com and as a print book customer, you are entitled to a discount on the eBook copy. Get in touch with us at customercare@packtpub.com for more details.

At www.packtpub.com, you can also read a collection of free technical articles, sign up for a range of free newsletters, and receive exclusive discounts and offers on Packt books and eBooks.

Other Books You May Enjoy

If you enjoyed this book, you may be interested in these other books by Packt:

Designing and Prototyping Interfaces with Figma

Fabio Staiano

ISBN: 978-1-83546-460-1

- Create high-quality designs that cater to your users' needs, providing an outstanding experience
- Mastering mobile-first design and responsive design concepts
- Integrate AI capabilities into your design workflow to boost productivity and explore design innovation
- Craft immersive prototypes with conditional prototyping and variables
- Communicate effectively to technical and non-technical audiences
- Develop creative solutions for complex design challenges
- Gather and apply user feedback through interactive prototypes

Express Your Creativity with Adobe Express

Rosie Sue

ISBN: 978-1-80323-774-9

- Learn how to create stunning social media graphics without having any prior design skills
- Repurpose graphic content and convert them to animations
- Create a beautiful responsive web page or marketing splash page, without coding knowledge
- Create once and repurpose the content in different aspect ratios for all the social media platforms
- Repurpose video for various social media uses and adhere to the aspect ratios for each platform
- Create compelling eye-catching content for your audience to engage with
- Create a landing page to collect leads

Packt is searching for authors like you

If you're interested in becoming an author for Packt, please visit `authors.packtpub.com` and apply today. We have worked with thousands of developers and tech professionals, just like you, to help them share their insight with the global tech community. You can make a general application, apply for a specific hot topic that we are recruiting an author for, or submit your own idea.

Share Your Thoughts

Now you've finished *Canva Cookbook*, we'd love to hear your thoughts! Scan the QR code below to go straight to the Amazon review page for this book and share your feedback or leave a review on the site that you purchased it from.

`https://packt.link/r/1-801-07530-1`

Your review is important to us and the tech community and will help us make sure we're delivering excellent quality content.

Download a free PDF copy of this book

Thanks for purchasing this book!

Do you like to read on the go but are unable to carry your print books everywhere?

Is your eBook purchase not compatible with the device of your choice?

Don't worry, now with every Packt book you get a DRM-free PDF version of that book at no cost.

Read anywhere, any place, on any device. Search, copy, and paste code from your favorite technical books directly into your application.

The perks don't stop there, you can get exclusive access to discounts, newsletters, and great free content in your inbox daily

Follow these simple steps to get the benefits:

1. Scan the QR code or visit the link below

https://packt.link/free-ebook/9781801075305

2. Submit your proof of purchase
3. That's it! We'll send your free PDF and other benefits to your email directly

www.ingramcontent.com/pod-product-compliance
Lightning Source LLC
Chambersburg PA
CBHW080623060326
40690CB00021B/4799